INSIDE LIFE:

I BEND,

I DON'T BREAK

SEYI OLUYOLE

Inside Life: I Bend, I Don't Break
Seyi Oluyole

© 2021

ISBN - 978-978-996-034-7

First Editor: Joy Ehonwa; joy.ehonwa@gmail.com; 08060753875
Second Editor and Book Publication Strategist: Damore Alli; dr2103.anonymous@gmail.com; 09083230774
Portrait Artist: Emmanuel Anaiye Ifebunmi; Dwerbartist (IG); www.artistemmanuel.com
Cover Design Artist: Everybees; everybees@gmail.com; 07065059986; everybees (IG)

Published by:
Heart2World Publishing
heart2worldpublishing.org
30, Muyiwa Opaleye,
Surulere, Lagos

For information on distribution, translation or bulk sales, please contact:

Seyi Oluyole
Phone (WhatsApp only): +2348185251889
Email: shembaseyi@gmail.com

For Nkiru Njoku

'I owe you my life' would seem like an exaggeration to
many;
I do.
I love you and I am eternally grateful.

*'I live my life day by day, and that's how I continue
to live it.'*
-    Naomi Campbell

INTRODUCTION

Writing this book is one of the most difficult things I have ever had to do. I've had to go back to places in my memory that I never wanted to visit again, stirring up pain and secrets locked up in the recesses of my mind. I've had to face my emotions, raw and sore, and come to a place of anguish, but also a place of understanding. I've had to face realities I had told myself did not exist.

I relieved this pain for myself, because I needed it; but also to help my sisters out there — the young women who love and are inspired by me, and would not in a million years have imagined that a person like me could be a victim of domestic violence. I mean, I'm a catch and any man lucky to be on my radar would treat me like a queen and protect me, right?

Well, this happened to me. I didn't ask for it but it did happen to me. And I feel a strong tug to tell my story — of how extremely lucky I am that I didn't become a statistic.

As I write this book, fear, anxiety, pain and worry assail me, but here is what I say to myself every time the doubt creeps in: 'You have to tell this story, Seyi. You *have* to.'

This is my story[1].

---

[1] *Disclosure: I have changed names of some persons referenced in this book, for the sake of protecting their privacies.*

CHAPTER ONE

THE BEGINNING OF THE END

"Lies don't end relationships, the truth does."
— Shannon L. Alder

Monday, July 8, 2019

3:40 a.m. (approximately)

I am awakened by an excruciating pain in my stomach. I am not a stranger to abdominal pain, having battled stomach ulcer for years, but this one is different. Usually, the ache would start and I would roll around my bed until the pain subsides or until I find sleep. But it is not the same this time. The pain doesn't subside and I am unable to sleep.

I look around my bedroom, hoping to feel the familiar arms of my lover around me. I realise I am alone in bed — my husband isn't by my side. This is not entirely strange. There have been times I would wake up in the middle of the night and find his side of the bed empty.

The first few times it happened, I went in search of him. I usually found him downstairs, somewhere in the 5-bedroom duplex we shared. He would say he went to make sure the gates were properly locked. Or that he was restless and overwhelmed by stress, his lack of funds, and stagnation in his clothing business, so he went downstairs to think. I had no reason to question those explanations; they were *legit*. Or so they seemed.

The pain is still very intense, so I sit up. I look around the room again and see that the Nike Slides I gifted him a few months after we began dating are by the side of the bed. The clothes he wore the day before hang loosely on the mosquito net hanger above our bed, as though aware they aren't meant to be there and his night dress lays limply on the bed, beside me. He isn't supposed to move around the house without his clothes. This is a conversation we had long before we got married. I have my foster kids in the house and it is inappropriate for him to walk around wearing just boxers or panties.

I stand up, bend over like an inverted letter L, and slowly walk to the bedroom door. As I open it, it makes a creaking noise I have become very familiar with. I have only taken a couple of steps down the stairs when he meets up with me. I am still clutching my stomach in pain.

'What is wrong? Is your stomach paining you?'

'Yes,' I respond as I let his warm hands hold my waist.

He begins to lead me back up the stairs. 'Maybe you should try to use the toilet.'

I have no objections. There have been times when my stomach pain would subside after a bowel movement.

He takes me to the bathroom. I pull down my panties and take a seat on the porcelain throne, letting my body adjust to its coldness.

He stands by the door, staring. Then he says, 'Sorry.'

I nod. I don't feel any relief and I sense something is out of place.

Just then, I see his left hand go towards his boxers. He starts to scratch his balls and I notice that he has an erection. Seeing that I notice, he quickly takes his hand off his boxers. My instincts grow stronger. Since when did he become shy about scratching in my presence?

'The clothes I put in the washing machine was just two minutes before I came. Let me quickly go and check, I am coming,' he says.

As he leaves, my suspicion that something is wrong does not leave with him.

Once I hear the door to our bedroom signal his exit, I stand up, pull up my panties, and head out to join him. I am almost at the bottom of the stairs when he rushes out to me again from the kitchen, stopping me from going down the stairs like the last time. He puts his hands on the silver railings of the stairs, preventing me from moving any further.

'You aren't using the toilet anymore?'

'I think I'll get some water,' I respond.

I push past the hands he placed on the railings and he reluctantly lets me through, following me to the kitchen. He offers to help me get the water and I watch as he pours 'pure' water into a transparent cup. As he takes salt and begins to pour it in the water, my heart tugs at me and my legs will me to move, to make sure nothing is wrong.

What could be wrong? Did he sneak a girl into the house at midnight?

I obey my heart and move to the back door; it is locked. I step out of the kitchen and walk towards the short corridor that leads to our guest room. The lights are off; we have no guests. I peep into the room without turning on the lights and walk away.

Next, I peep into the opposite room, which we use as a store. It is filled with clothes and mattresses, nothing out of the ordinary. I want to go back to the kitchen but my legs move me up the stairs; my heart agrees.

I go up the stairs and walk past our bedroom, straight down the corridor to the room where my foster daughters sleep. I open the door. They are all sound asleep but one of the girls isn't at her sleeping spot. I open their bathroom and the light shines back at me as the vacant toilet seat mocks me; she isn't there either. I head back to the kitchen where my husband is.

'I can't find Blessing,' I say.

He doesn't seem bothered.

'Did you hear me? I said I can't find Blessing.'

'Ah!' The exclamation is as fake as the ground on which I stand is real. 'Did you check the bathroom?' he adds.

'Yes, she isn't there.'

He just points at the glass of water. 'Drink, so you can feel better.'

I remember, then, that it was a crazy stomach pain that had woken me up. My body is beginning to shiver. Blessing is nowhere to be found.

I run back to the girls' room and check her sleeping area for the phone I gave her. It isn't there. I have an idea.

I go to our room, pick up my phone, and head back downstairs. I dial the number saved on my phone as 'Children'. It begins to ring from the guest room. I wait.

Then, Blessing emerges from the guest room, an exaggerated sleepy look plastered on her face.

'What were you doing in there?'

'I was reading, then I fell asleep, Ma.'

'Reading how? I came in there and the lights were off.'

Silence.

I walk towards the guest room and turn on the lights.

'Where is the book you were reading and how come the lights were off if you were truly reading?'

'I was reading, Ma.' She has a resolute look on her face.

I feel the pain in my stomach again and my legs become weak. I hope that what I am thinking isn't what it is, but my knees can no longer carry me. I sit on one of the chairs by the corridor.

'Can you explain to me how you were reading and slept off in the guest room when there are no books here and the room light was off?'

'Ma, I was reading here then I went inside… when I was feeling sleepy.'

'You are lying, Blessing.'

'No, Ma. I was reading. I came down at around 3:30 to read, then I read small and fell asleep.'

'Did you see me?' My husband's voice comes from behind me.

She looks at him and shakes her head.

I'm not sure if I am running mad. Is my mind messing with me again?

'Blessing, I was down here at about 3:45 so what time did you read?' I ask.

'Your stomach is paining you,' my husband says. 'Let's go upstairs first. We can resolve this later.'

He pulls me off the chair and leads me upstairs. I do not object. When we get back to our bedroom, he goes to pee. As he comes back into the room, I spring back on my feet.

'Something's not right,' I say to him, then head back downstairs. By this time, Blessing is in the kitchen. Before I can say a word to her, my husband is back in the kitchen with us.

'I'd like to talk to her alone,' I say to him.

He looks from me to her. His stare at her lingers for a few seconds, then he walks away.

I sit on the kitchen stool as I become aware of my stomach pain again.

'Blessing, you are lying to me. Tell me what you were doing downstairs,' I say to her.

'I am not lying, Ma. I was reading, then I slept off.'

'What you are saying is not adding up. Your timeline is scattered. There was no book in the room and the lights were off. Tell me the truth, Blessing.'

She hesitates for a few seconds. 'That is what happened, Ma.'

This back and forth goes on for 45 minutes. Her words do not change, and although I want to believe her, my instincts are pushing very strong. At some point during this exchange, my husband comes into the kitchen with a fake sleepy face.

'When are you coming to bed?'

'We are not done,' I respond.

He nods, gives Blessing another lingering stare, and leaves.

I am no detective but I sure as hell know that something isn't right. I take a deep breath. Then, I remind my 19-year-old foster child, Blessing, that I have taken care of her since she was 14.

'This is your chance to tell me the truth, Blessing. Whatever you say, I will believe you. Once I walk out of this kitchen, your chance to come clean is gone. I will believe what anyone says over you.'

She stares at the floor, a frown slowly taking over her face. 'I came downstairs. I saw *Daddy Yo*. We were talking and when I heard the sound of your door, I ran to hide.'

My heart skips a beat. My anxiety starts to rear its head as my stomach begins to hurt again. *Be still*, I say to myself.

'Why would you run away when you heard me coming down?'

'Because I don't want you to think there is something between me and *Daddy Yo*.'

My heart begins to beat faster.

Be still, Seyi.

'Why would I think there is something between you two?'

Silence.

She looks down at her feet.

Be still.

'So what were you two talking about?'

'He asked when I will start my exams and if Mr. Solanke has told me that GCE form is out.'

I stare at her. I know she is still lying. I know there is a lot more. But I also cannot recognize her — this is not the girl I would have trusted with my life, once upon a time.

'Is there anything else?'

She shakes her head.

'Tell me now. This is your chance.'

She shakes her head again.

'Okay. Thank you, Blessing.'

She turns to leave. My life is about to undergo a major turnaround.

*

I enter the bedroom I share with the man I am married to. I can't remember his exact position but I do remember we are both sitting on the bed when I say, 'Blessing said she was talking to you.'

Confusion and shock take over his face all at once.

'Me? She was talking to me?'

'Yes.'

'I wasn't talking to her. I didn't even see her.'

'Well, she said she was talking to you about her exams.'

He shakes his head and lets out a chuckle, still looking quite confused. 'You are sure that's what she said? Let me go and ask her.'

He gets off the bed and I follow him. I head over to the girls' room and call Blessing to come out to us at the corridor. He stands at the door to our room, frowning, while Blessing stands by the railings.

'You said we were talking downstairs? That you saw me?'

'Yes, Sir.'

He waits for a beat, then repeats his question. She answers in the affirmative. He looks genuinely bewildered and I am also becoming baffled.

'What were we talking about?' he asks her, still disconcerted.

'You were asking me about my exam and if Mr. Solanke said GCE form is ready.'

He opens his mouth in shock and immediately turns to me. 'I asked her that question on Friday after me and you discussed it in the kitchen.'

'Me and you did not discuss that in the kitchen on Friday,' I say.

'We did when we were washing plates,' he insists.

We were talking about Blessing's exams while washing plates but I am very sure we did not discuss the form being out. 'No, we did not,' I insist.

We are both quiet for a minute. I really just want to know what exactly is going on; which of them is seeing a ghost.

'You can go, Blessing,' he dismisses her.

This isn't his first attempt at confusing me and muddling details, but I am sure about this because

Blessing's exams are the most important thing to me at the moment.

Back in our bedroom, he looks at me with puzzled eyes. 'I don't understand what is happening. Why would Blessing say she saw me when I didn't see her?'

'I don't know, but I really want answers.'

He attempts to convince me that he and I had spoken about Blessing's examination form being out the previous week, and tries to suggest that Blessing is probably confused. I doubt that she is confused, and I tell him this.

We are quiet for a few minutes as I try to move through the cloud that has gathered in my brain. I make no assumptions. I just want to know what exactly is happening.

He breaks the silence. 'Or did you tell her to be monitoring me?'

'Why would I ask her to do so?'

'I don't know. I'm just wondering why she would say she saw me when she didn't.'

'I am wondering the same too.'

At this point, my curiosity is heightened. Normally, I would move on; but this time, it is difficult. There is no way to explain this situation.

He turns to me again. 'Or did you tell her about the false rape case I told you about?'

'No. Why would I?'

'I don't know. I wish the CCTV was still working so that I can show you that I did not even see her or talk to her.'

I have no response.

We go quiet again, but then he starts to mumble, like he is trying to understand what is happening. I am not mumbling, but I am still perplexed.

'Who do you even believe? Are you saying you trust her over your husband?' he breaks the silence again.

'I don't trust or believe anyone. I just want to know the exact truth because I am confused.'

'I am too.'

I can see his manipulative eyes, begging me to believe him and take his word for it like I have done a million times before. But the truth is what I need.

He jumps off the bed. 'I want to talk to her again. '

'Okay.'

I follow him as he heads out. I walk to the girls' room. It's already 6 a.m. and the younger girls are taking their baths and preparing for school. I find Blessing behind the door.

'Are you sure you saw *Daddy Yo* downstairs?' I ask her.

'Yes, Ma,' she says with a hint of fear and confidence.

'Can you swear on your mother's life that you saw him and you were talking?'

'Yes, Ma,' her confidence doesn't waver but her fear becomes palpable.

'Okay. Come with me.'

We walk out of the room, through the corridor, to where he is standing.

'I would like to talk to her alone,' he says.

I refuse.

'But when you said you wanted to talk to her alone downstairs, I let you.'

'That is different. It was a woman to woman talk. Whatever you want to say to her, say it here where I can hear.'

He insists that he really needs to speak with her privately but I am too smart to agree to this. When he sees that I won't give them privacy, he tells her she can go. Then, he heads back to our bedroom.

I don't follow him this time. At this point, I am very convinced there is something going on. I don't want it to be true, but I can't change reality.

*

8 a.m.

The children are ready to go to school, and I see them off to the gate like I always do. As I turn to head back inside, I see my husband walk towards me with a smug look on his face. He is wearing a white vest that I gave him as a gift, and the three-quarter shorts I got him for his last birthday. I recall for a brief moment that my supposed lover and husband bought me nothing for my last birthday, but I remind myself that I have bigger issues.

I walk away like he isn't there, but he pulls me back and I stop, allowing him to lead me to the corridor. I step in first. He follows and sits on the brown couch we put there. I remain standing while he calls for Blessing, who appears almost immediately, as though she has been waiting.

I wonder if he finally spoke to her privately, but I don't have to speculate long. He begins to speak, his voice low and raspy, yet confident. He sounds like he is picking every word carefully, making sure he doesn't say the wrong thing.

'It's true that I saw Blessing,' he says.

The stomach pain returns and I start to shiver. I try to stay calm, to listen to the rest of his explanation.

'When I saw her, she asked where you were and I told her you were sleeping. Then, she said she was scared that if you came out and saw both of us talking, you would suspect us. And I asked her the meaning of that. I was even annoyed, but I just left her and went to the kitchen.'

I look at Blessing. 'So, you went to hide, because...?'

'It's because when I came down from the staircase, *Daddy Yo* was talking to me but he was wearing only boxers. And I was scared because I have not seen his boxers before. So, when you opened the door, I ran to hide.'

I look from this girl who has obviously been manipulated, to the disgusting shameless man I am married to. I let out a short laugh. Then, I ask her to leave.

I regard him, blankly; my laughter, gone. My heart is heavy with the pain of betrayal.

'You lie to me a lot and I act stupid, like I don't know what is going on. But this is too much and I'm done with this marriage.'

As I start to walk away, he tries to pull me back, but I evade his grasp and head into the house.

In retrospect, I should have headed out of the house.

CHAPTER TWO

TO LOVE AND TO HURT, TILL DEATH DO US 'PART

"They provoke you but when you defend yourself, they cry victim."
— Mitta Xinindlu

I am in our spare room.

Before I move here, he tries to convince me that there is nothing between him and Blessing, and it was all a misunderstanding.

'You lied from 3:40 a.m. to 8:00 a.m.'

'I wanted to know if you had told Blessing something about me.'

His lies have become so weak and disgusting, they sound like an insult to my intelligence.

Prior to this incident, two of my girls won a trip to Egypt, as player escorts for the AFCON 2019, one of the biggest moments I have been waiting for. The trip, scheduled for July 10th - 12th 2019, requires a guardian for each travelling child, so my husband and I opt to travel as guardians to the girls.

We need yellow cards to travel.

I give Blessing a copy of my yellow card and ask her to go to the nearest health centre to inquire if they issue such cards. Before she leaves, I ask her if there are more details about 'them' that she hasn't told me yet. She says no.

I await her return in the spare room, still extremely upset. I want out of the marriage. We have been married for nine months and I have not had a full month of happiness.

I start to text my lawyer, Samuel. I tell him I have a friend who would like to dissolve her marriage on the grounds that she caught her husband having an affair with their maid. While I chat with him, my husband comes into the room and sits by my side. He continues trying to convince me that there is nothing between him and Blessing. I move away from him.

My phone beeps a number of times as Samuel replies my messages. I do not look at the messages. I do not want him to peep and see them. When he notices my reservation, he attempts to snatch my phone. I react quickly and dodge his reaching hands. We struggle.

Soon, I fall to the ground, still guarding my phone from his grasp. He wrestles me on the floor, and my strength is no match for his. He overpowers me and takes the phone.

He begins to read the messages I have sent to Samuel, while I sit on the floor, watching him helplessly.

'Cheating? Having an affair?' he asks as he reads.

'Give me my phone!'

'No. This is my evidence. You are lying against me.'

I start to feel bad; I am believing him again. He looks pained, like I am accusing him wrongly. But I still want my phone back.

I attempt to take it from him, but he raises his arm out of reach. I am like a child playing 'jumper' with an adult. I jump, trying to pull his arms down to get my phone; I do not succeed. He is taller and stronger. I keep trying till he leaves the room. I follow him. I am upset that he is bullying me.

My frustration builds and I begin to cry. When I hear Blessing come back from the errand I sent her on, I try again.

'Give me the phone before Blessing comes around,' I demand.

He knows I hate having arguments when the kids are around. He uses this knowledge to his advantage and continues to keep my phone hostage. I have no plans of backing down.

'They don't have the yellow card,' Blessing tells me.

'Okay, thank you.'

She leaves, and we resume the tussle. He would hold the phone far out of my reach; I would chase, plead, cry, fight, surrender and replay.

Blessing comes around the staircase when she hears me crying. Two of my young girls who are yet to resume school are with her.

'Please *Daddy Yo*, give her the phone, please,' she begs him.

'She is saying I am sleeping with you. Imagine that, Blessing.'

Blessing does not deny or affirm this claim. She goes uncomfortably quiet.

'Blessing, please take the girls to another room. I don't want them to see this!' I yell through my sobs.

'If you leave that place, I will slap you,' he says.

Blessing stays put.

'Princess and Silver, go and hide somewhere,' I say. The younger girls run off while Blessing stays.

I continue to jostle, yell, cry and beg for my phone.

My leg hits a mop stick. I pick it up in frustration and throw it aside. The mop stick breaks.

'Can you see, Blessing? She broke the mop stick on my leg! Stay o, Blessing, because you will be my witness.'

'The mop stick did not even touch you.' I state, incredulously-- my throat, dry from all the yelling and crying.

He heads for the staircase and launches down the flight of stairs. I hold on to his shirt and it begins to rip.

'You are tearing what I'm wearing,' he says to me in Yoruba.

'Give me my phone so I can leave your clothes alone.'

He is a stubborn bully. He refuses to yield.

'You're ripping my shirt,' he complains again.

'I bought it for you as a birthday gift,' I remind him, 'even though you gave me nothing for my birthday.'

He continues to launch forward. I am losing my hold on him.

He stops midway down, turns to me and starts mumbling to himself. He shakes his head, soon after, like he is convincing himself against an idea. Then, he charges down the remaining flight of stairs. I let go of him to avoid getting hurt but I run after him, nonetheless.

In the living room turned dance studio, I grab him again.

'Give me my phone!'

He raises it out of my reach. I try to hit him in his balls to weaken him, but I don't succeed. He attempts to tackle me to the ground. I manoeuvre the first time, but the second time, I fall and land on my back.

He puts his hands around my neck as if to choke me. *'Ma fe pa e!'* I will almost kill you.

I feel defeated at this point, so I stay down. As soon as he stands and heads out with my phone, I find new strength to jump up and run after him. He opens his car, throws my phone inside, and locks it before I can stop him.

I turn to see my two younger girls watching us in confusion.

'Hide!' I yell to them as I follow him back inside. 'Give me back my phone!'

Blessing is still watching from the stairs and it occurs to me to give her some money to take the girls out.

'Blessing, bring me my wallet.'

When she returns with my wallet, he tries to get it from her. I attempt to beat him to it but he pushes me to the wall and pins my neck there with his forearm as he snatches the wallet from her.

He heads out and throws the wallet in his car.

I resume my tears. 'Why have you seized my wallet and my phone? Why?'

He ignores me and heads upstairs. I follow him. I am exhausted but determined, so I start to yell again. 'Give my phone back to me!'

He goes into the spare room where I had been, earlier, and takes my other phone.

'What did I do? Why are you taking my other phone?'

He ignores me as he adds the phone to his earlier collection in the car. I continue to cry, cursing myself for ever letting him into my life and the lives of the kids.

He comes back upstairs and goes to our bedroom. He picks up an empty water bottle and takes water from the dispenser. When he tries to drink it, I hit the water bottle and the water spills.

He turns to me with a dark stare. 'You are inviting the Devil.'

I am frightened. I do not hit the water bottle again. I watch him blankly as he drinks the water, asking myself how I got here.

Once he has quenched his thirst, he turns to me with a bright smile and starts to tug at my cheeks. I slap his hands off but he doesn't stop.

'Baby girl,' he coos.

Then, he heads to the door, locks it, and puts the key in his pocket.

My orange shirt is soaked from sweat but I no longer care. All the fight in me is gone; I stare blankly at him. He pushes me to the bed and makes me sit.

'Please open the door, I want to go out.'

'No.'

He tells me how he has always dreamed of having a great marriage and how he can't be a failure by having a failed marriage. He goes to the corridor and calls for Blessing. Then, he heads out of the room and locks me inside.

A few minutes later, I hear whispers. I walk to the door and put my ear against it, but I can't figure out what they are talking about. They stop talking and I run back to the bed.

When he re-enters the room, he is holding the large bottle of Sniper I had bought a week ago to exterminate bed bugs. I know what this means but I try not to think about it.

He sits on the bed and places the Sniper on the floor beside him.

'Please open the door. I need to go and print our tickets for the Egypt trip.'

'No, we can do that later.'

He shows me the Sniper and says, 'This is our drink.'

I shake my head. 'It is not my drink.'

'You know how I used to say let's commit suicide together? Let's do it today,' he says to me.

'I am not ready to die.'

My heart is racing as I wonder what the world would think happened if I die. I think about Jessica, my very good friend and Deborah, my family friend whom I have known since when I was five and she was three. These two are my closest friends, whom I'd tell almost anything, and I wish I can send them a message saying, *If anything happens to me, I did not commit suicide.*

After a few minutes, he kneels beside me and says he wants us to start afresh. I regard him mindlessly as he makes empty promises of being a great husband, the best husband ever.

I want to object, refuse; I want to tell him I want no part of it, but I have no fight left in me.

'Baby Girl. That is what I will start calling you now.' He pulls me up and starts to kiss me. My body does not respond.

'I think we should take a shower.'

He takes off my sweat-soaked clothes and ushers me to the bathroom where we both take a shower. I feel numb through it all.

After the shower, he leads me back to the bed where he starts to kiss me and caress my body. He stops when he sees that I am not responding.

'You don't look like you want this.'

'I do,' I say, quietly.

He continues, applies some oil on his penis and penetrates me.

I lay with my eyes wide open as he goes in and out, whispering sweet nothings. A lone tear falls, and I quickly hold back the waterworks waiting to follow. I don't know what he will do if he sees me crying.

He eventually comes inside me, and pulls me into his arms as he falls asleep.

I doze off for a few minutes.

When I open my eyes, I go into the bathroom to clean up and notice that he has left the key at the door. I know this is my chance. I quickly put on my clothes, and head to the other room.

I curl into a foetal position on the bed, trying to understand — and forget — all that has just happened. I drift off.

A few minutes later, I am awakened by whispers. It is him and Blessing again. I hear them talking by the stairs. Blessing peeps into my room and sees that my eyes are open. She goes on her knees.

'I am sorry I ran away when I heard you coming,' she says.

I have no strength left. I nod. She stands and leaves.

*

I am still lying on the bed in the spare room thinking of a way out. I do not have my phones or my wallet. My laptop is beside me but I do not touch it. I am afraid he will seize this too.

I do not know his game plan but I do not want him seizing my MacBook Air, my most prized possession, which I worked very hard to purchase last year.

He comes to the door. He has *that smile* again; it looks scary to me now.

'I have a surprise for you,' he says.

I shake my head. I have had enough surprises for the day.

'Come to the room. I have a surprise for you.'

I don't want to stand up.

He comes to me and pulls me up. He leads me to our bedroom, and I follow like an obedient child.

When I enter the room, I stay by the door. He stands behind me.

'Look on the bedside table, I have something for you there.'

I walk to the bedside table. There is no surprise. I turn back to him.

He smiles. 'I have no surprise.' Then, he locks the door again.

I accept my fate and sit on the bed.

He walks towards me. 'I can't bear the thought of a failed marriage. All my life, I have planned on how to have a perfect family. A perfect life. I don't want you to leave me.'

I do not respond. It begins to dawn on me that I deserve better than this man who takes my money, sleeps with a girl I take care of, and also bullies me.

He continues talking, but I am no longer listening. My mind is muddled up.

Suddenly, he pushes me onto the bed, pinning my hands beneath my buttocks as he straddles me.

I start to cry. 'Please don't kill me.'

He stares at me. Then, shakes his head. 'I would never kill you,' he says.

But I don't know what is true and what is false with him anymore. I think about Jessica again. I wish I can send her a telepathic message: *Jessica, I did not kill myself.*

He takes a pillow and puts it by my side. He looks at the pillow, then at me, picks up the pillow and throws it over my face. I shake my head vigorously until the pillow falls off and I am looking at him again. His eyes are vacant. I do not know this man sitting astride me. Did I ever know him?

He smiles again and gets off me. I sit up.

Then, he resumes his apologetic speech, begging me not to leave and promising to be a better husband, the best husband in the world.

The promises stink of rust — from overuse and unfulfillment.

He holds my hands and attempts to make a puppy face. I wonder if he is sincere this time. I also wonder whom I will tell about my ordeal.

Niran, the Visa staff in charge of our sponsored Egypt trip, crosses my mind. He had asked me out to lunch before. *Niran would probably not treat me like this if I were married to him. Maybe if I leave this marriage, I can get Niran to ask me out on a date again. Then, I'll have a better man.*

My sister crosses my mind too. Today is the Monday she won't be coming over to spend the night. Then, I think about Deborah; we haven't spoken in a while. Will she miss me when I am gone? Over my thoughts, I hear his promises that I have refused to take to heart this time. Everything hurts so much. I don't want to be with him anymore. But I can't say it out loud. I am afraid for my life.

I ask him for my phone.

He pushes me to the bed again, pins my hands beneath my buttocks and straddles me, like the last time. I wonder if this is it.

He throws the pillow at my face again and I begin to shiver.

'I won't leave you!' I yell. 'We can make it work.'

'Are you sure?'

'Yes.'

This goes on for hours -- my assurance, his confirmation. I continue to agree with him that we can make it work. The time is somewhere around 4 p.m. I know this because my kids are back from school. I am so ashamed to face them in my condition. I wonder how Princess and Silver feel. I hope that I have not scarred them for life.

When my kids knock at the door, asking to see me and of my whereabouts, he does not let me respond. He whispers a response to them at the door and turns them away, casually. I would later find out he told them I wasn't feeling well.

At about 6 p.m., he takes my phones from the dressing table and hands them to me. I feel a little stupid that I hadn't seen them there earlier. I see that I have a missed call from Niran.

I call him back.

'Why didn't you pick your call?' he asks.

'I forgot my phone at home,' I lie.

'I wanted to stop by to give you the kids' Visa shirts.' He had offered to make customized shirts with the girls' names on them for the Egypt trip. But it is too late now, so we agree that he will find another way to give them to the kids before the trip.

I go to my WhatsApp to read the messages Samuel sent. I apologise for the break in communication. I want to tell him all that happened but I am scared Crazy Man will find out. When Crazy Man looks away, I quickly share some details with Samuel. I delete the chats as I send them.

Crazy Man looks at me and asks who I am chatting with.

'No one,' I tell him.

'I saw you typing a message.'

I deny it. 'I was not.'

I have deleted the messages from my end so there is no way for him to confirm.

Someone knocks again. It's Phave, my nephew, who has been ill for a few days. He wants to see me. Crazy Man doesn't let Phave see me. He tells him I am resting.

When he shuts the door, I beg him to let me take Phave to the hospital. Surprisingly, he agrees, and offers to drop us off in his car.

Outside the room, I am glad to have my freedom again. My eyes are swollen from crying all day. My kids are happy to see me. They tell me 'sorry' and ask if I'm feeling better. I want to tell them that I am not sick but I don't. I realise this is what he told them.

I walk out of the house with my swollen eyes, Phave behind me. Crazy Man is already outside, and has opened the car door. I am riding shotgun.

Just then, he says he needs to get something and heads back inside.

I am relieved to be rid of him for a few minutes. I quickly update Samuel on the condition of my 'friend'. I tell him how her husband put a pillow over her face and tried to get her to drink Sniper.

I delete the messages as I send them.

He comes back outside.

When I see his face, I feel warmth. I feel pity. I don't think I should leave him. I am worried about how broken he will be if I do.

I have no one to share these colliding thoughts with, so I go on Twitter and tweet *'I don't know how to care for myself. Someone could threaten/attempt to kill me and I'd still feel pity for them right after.'*

At the hospital, I purchase a registration card and accompany Phave to stations where nurses run a series of tests on him. He hasn't had a proper meal all day; the nurses say I should get him something to eat. I decide to get something for him from my usual bakery, which is nearby. Crazy Man insists on coming with me. We walk there in silence.

When I complete my purchase, the attendant, who is always happy to see me, asks why my eyes are so swollen and whether I am ill.

'She will be fine,' my husband says before I can respond.

I pay, collect my change, and we leave.

I continue to chat with Samuel at the hospital, while I wait for Phave to be attended to. He keeps saying my friend needs to leave the house. I make excuses about why she cannot leave. They have a business trip; it will break his heart.

Crazy Man gets up and says he needs to take a walk. I am relieved to be free of him even if it's for a few minutes.

While he is gone, I continue my conversation with Samuel. Suddenly, something catches my eye. There is a strange notification icon on my phone. I click on it and it says my WhatsApp is connected to a desktop. I quickly log out from the desktop but I know what has happened. He has hacked into my WhatsApp and is reading my messages to Samuel.

I realise I am in deep shit and I can't think of a way to get myself out. If I run away now, what happens to my kids at home? I decide to pretend like I don't know what he has done.

When we return home, he heads upstairs. I stay downstairs; I don't want to be near him. I haven't eaten all day and I need to make myself something to eat. I warm some stew and rice. My throat is very dry. I need water.

But there is no 'pure' water in the kitchen and the water dispenser is in our room upstairs, so I have to go there. When I get to the top of the stairs, I see him in the spare room working on my MacBook. He has *that smile* on his face.

I turn toward our room. As soon as I take the water from the dispenser, he enters. I do not think to run. I am certain he won't lock me up again; he has already apologised.

He gives me *that smile*. I sip water from my cup.

'You are still planning on leaving me.'

I start to shake my head.

'I saw your WhatsApp messages to the lawyer.'

Shit.

With this confirmation that he was indeed the one who hacked into my WhatsApp, I know I have to figure out an escape plan. I don't want him to kill me now that he knows I still have plans to leave.

He turns to lock the door again. I set the cup down, my heart in my mouth. I am trying to think of a way out. I can't scream. I have to keep my kids safe. I don't want to do anything that would make him take them hostage or harm them. I don't want them to see or know any more of what is happening.

I don't want him to kill me.

He pulls me to the bed, and like a sheep to the slaughter, I follow him.

'I want to spend one last moment with you.'

He lies down beside me and wraps his arms around me. He starts to talk about dying with me by his side. I am very freaked out by the idea of a man dying by my side. I try to leave the bed, to release myself from his grip; it is futile.

I start to cry again as I beg him to let me go. I kick and writhe, I exert my waning strength.

He eventually loosens his grip and says, 'I am weak. I will soon go, don't worry.'

I ask him what he took. I want to call his mother or sister to tell them that their child is trying to commit suicide. He seizes my phones again. I stand up from the bed and beg him to let me out of the room.

His voice is weak, like he is about to die. He holds his chest, then his arms, he tells me again that he is getting weak and he needs me by his side. My grief is amplified. My cry becomes a wail, I wonder why my kids can't hear me.

I question God, then myself. Why am I so unfortunate in life? Why are so many terrible things happening at the verge of my breakthrough?

'Stop being dramatic,' he tells me.

I realise he doesn't know the depth of my anguish. He thinks it is all an act.

'Please slap me or punch me,' I beg him. I need an outlet for these growing pains. He doesn't.

I attempt to retrieve my phones, which he had thrown under the bed, but he overpowers and stops me. This is when I realise that he is not dying. He is only trying to manipulate me mentally.

'Why are you doing this to me? Why are you acting this way? Have I offended you?' I ask him.

'You are planning to leave me.'

'I am not leaving you. I told you already,' I lie desperately. 'I knew you were reading my messages that is why I tried to mislead you while talking to the lawyer.'

I don't know if he believes me.

'I'm only doing all this because I love you. I don't want to lose you,' he says.

'You are behaving like a coward. A true man would work towards winning his wife back, not lock her up.'

'I'm sorry. Forgive me, please. I can't stand losing you.'

I really want him to let me go. I remind him of how every man that I have met, other than my brothers and father, has hurt me in every way possible. 'I always thought you would be the one man to change the dynamic,' I finish.

'I'm the one man. I love you.'

He sits up on the bed, demurely; his words, gentle like the break of dawn. If only he hadn't shown me the beast earlier. He apologises for the umpteenth time, and talks about loving me. Then, he blames me for his failures, for every bad thing that has ever happened to him.

My stomach pains return. It's my ulcer rearing its head again. I haven't eaten all day.

'I'm hungry. Please open the door for me so I can go get food.'

'No. There's cereal here for you to munch on.'

'I need real food. Not honey bunches of oats,' I tell him.

'Sorry, that's your problem,' he says, quietly.

I remind him of my ulcer, how important it is for me to eat. I stare into his eyes to find some emotion — some pity. They are blank.

I shake my head. The pain is unbearable.

The gentleman goes to hide and the beast comes out again.

He pushes me to the bed, and straddles me for the third time that day.

My fear is back.

He stares at me for a few seconds. Then, he takes the pillow and places it on my face again, for the third time that day; only this time, he applies pressure. I cry and yell; I shake my head to get the pillow off. It is futile.

Five seconds, six seconds — an eternity for me.

'TOBA IT'S ME SEYI!' I muffle into the pillow.

He takes the pillow off my face.

I weep — louder and stronger than I have done all day.

'Shhhhhh...' he says.

I quickly try to control my tears so he doesn't get upset and pick up the pillow again. He chuckles. He thinks it is funny that he is trying to suffocate me with a pillow.

I think about my life. I remember when I got pregnant the year before and how we couldn't have the baby because the circumstances were not right to start a family — he did not yet have a meaningful source of income and my finances were doing too much, too soon; that it did not make sense to add another mouth to the family payroll. For the first time, I am grateful we did not.

'I am so glad the baby did not live,' I say to him.

'That baby destroyed my life,' he says, still sitting on me.

I am nauseated by his comment because, frankly, I don't remember him ever having a life. Besides, how can a baby we never had destroy his life?

His weight on me is becoming uncomfortable. I beg him to stand up. He refuses.

'I promise I won't run off, please.'

The tears from my eyes run down my cheeks, into my ears.

My ears itch but he is sitting on my hands, so I am helpless.

'Please let me scratch my ears, please,' I beg him.

'No.'

'Please, I will let you sit back on me, I promise.'

He hesitates, then gets off me. I scratch my ear.

He starts to apologise again.

'My life is so unbelievable,' I tell him. 'It is like a story I would read on Twitter.'

'I saw what you wrote on Twitter earlier. If this ever gets on Twitter, I will be very angry.'

I have witnessed his anger today and I don't want to see it again. I make a mental note not to ever post this experience on Twitter.

It is 10 p.m. — the kids have come to remind me of the bedtime prayers.

'Can I have the keys? I want to say our night prayer with the kids.'

'Tell them to pray without you.'

'You guys go and pray,' I call out to the kids.

I turn to see him on the bed, unbothered; and it occurs to me that my hysteria is feeding him and making him stronger. I wipe my tears and practice deep breaths to hold back any new pools from forming in my eyes, then I return to the bed with a book, which I pretend to read.

I remember that I usually take my birth control pills at 10 p.m.

'I need to take my birth control. It's downstairs.'

'No, we do not need birth control anymore.'

I know what this means, but God forbid that I have a child by this monster.

I sit with my book and stare at the pages, quietly.

'I see that you have calmed down,' he says.

I ignore him and continue to read.

He stands, opens the door and walks out of the room.

My bones feel weak, my eyes are heavy, and my stomach hurts. I decide, then, that I need to sleep. I lay on the bed and soon enough, I drift off.

I feel someone tap me awake. It is him.

'Come and eat,' he says.

I don't want to eat anymore. I have become one with the pain of hunger. I try to go back to sleep but he does not let me. I eventually sit up.

'Would you like us to eat together?' He has *that smile* again.

I shake my head vehemently. I wait for him to say that is the only condition for eating. Instead, he laughs and says okay.

He escorts me downstairs.

I hope to get a glimpse of my kids but they have all gone to bed. I make the food, and eat a few spoons just to stop the stomach pain.

Then, he leads me back upstairs. My eyes catch my birth control pills, sitting on the table underneath the stairs. I need a plan to get them.

When we get to the top of the stairs and he is now by my side, I say, 'I forgot something.'

I run downstairs before he can stop me and grab the packet. I hide it in my pocket, then head back upstairs. His eyes are on me. I hope that he didn't see me take the pill.

He leads us back to the room and locks the door. We are both silent.

A few minutes later, I tell him I need to use the bathroom. Once I am by myself, I pop a pill into my mouth.

Then I take out my phone and write a poem for myself:

I deserve so much!
So much more than this
Somehow, every man I have met
Has broken me
Bit by bit.
Leaving me more tattered than the last.
Now, I am a shadow of myself

CHAPTER THREE

THE UNCLES AND THE CHILD

"The silence was killing me.
And that's all there ever was. Silence. It was all I
knew. Keep quiet. Pretend nothing had happened,
that nothing was wrong. And look how well that was
turning out."
— J. Lynn

I don't remember the first time or the first uncle.

I may not even remember all the uncles because these are memories that I have long forgotten and buried in the quiet depths of my mind.

But I'll start with Brother Endurance and Brother Nduka, brothers whose father owned a pepper soup joint, and were friends to my brother. Brother Nduka is the older one. His dark skin, a perplexing contrast to his brother's light complexion. They often had reasons to visit our house.

I remember Brother Nduka showing me his penis and making me rub it and put it in my mouth. Brother Endurance would say, 'Let us do mummy and daddy' and then he would show me what mummy and daddy do. On some days, I did not want to do mummy and daddy but being home alone when he came visiting made it impossible to decline his invitation.

I preferred when Brother Nduka visited; he was gentler and nicer, and didn't smell so bad. Brother Endurance was rough. It always felt painful when he touched my genitals and tried to force his fingers inside.

Many times, I tried to avoid them, but they knew the right time to invade my privacy without getting caught: after school when my older brothers were not home, or on Saturdays when my brothers had gone to the game house and my sister was at choir rehearsals.

I never told anyone. I didn't know I was meant to tell anyone.

*

Then, there was Uncle Danladi. He was the children's church teacher that year — very nice, the best children's church teacher we ever had.

He soon became friends with my brothers, who at the time were popular in the neighbourhood of our estate. He would visit our house every now and then.

The first day Uncle Danladi came, I was wearing the pair of green shorts Aunt Pamela had gifted me. They were my popular favourite. I would wear them almost all the time.

I was standing by the staircase of the block of flats that led to our apartment with Uncle Danladi and my friend, Tunrayo when he asked Tunrayo to get him some water. Once she left, he asked me to move closer. Then, he put his hands inside my shorts and inside my panties, and rubbed me. It was painful. A few seconds later, Tunrayo rushed out with the water and he took out his hands.

That was the last time I ever wore those shorts.

*

Brother Silas used to live with us. He used to sell barbecued chicken. He was like an uncle to me. One day, I stole one of his barbecued chickens and took it to school to share with my friends. The second time I tried to steal from him, he caught me and warned me off. I promised him I would never do it again. If my mum found out, I would be dead.

One day, while inspecting his chicken in the freezer, he called for me. I was worried someone had stolen more chicken and I was about to face the consequences of their misdeed because I had done it first.

'Do you know how to kiss?'

That was the question he called me for.

'No,' I responded.

'Okay, let me show you. There is short kiss and long kiss.' He moved closer and kissed me with his tongue in my mouth.

'That is short kiss. I will teach you long kiss another day.'

I nodded and left.

Two days later, I was home alone when he returned from the market. He called me into the bedroom and said it was time for the long kiss. We lived in a two-bedroom apartment at the time; my parents occupied one of the rooms, and the rest of us occupied the other. I wanted to say no, but I didn't want him to tell Mummy about the chicken.

So, he pulled me close and started to kiss me. It was a painfully long kiss and he almost swallowed my tongue. He squeezed the small 'koko' I had on my chest — they had not developed enough to be called breasts.

He stopped to ask if I liked it. I nodded. He wanted to try again.

'Please, I need to go and pee,' I begged him; he let me go.

I ran to the neighbour's house and sat there. He came out some minutes later, accusing me of leaving dirty plates in the kitchen.

'I'm giving you 10 minutes to come here and wash those plates, or else!'

I did not go. The kiss was too painful and my chest was hurting from the roughness of his hands.

I would avoid him, ever since.

*

On the bus, on our way from a school excursion, I remember being seated when someone's hand groped my thighs — it was a senior's hand. I did not stop him; it had become the norm for me.

He soon slid his hands into my panties.

*

Everyone would say I am beautiful; dark and pretty. I knew that my beauty was the cause of my woes. So, I became self-conscious and started to make myself unattractive. I would walk and dress like a boy — skirts and dresses made it easier for them to put their hands under. In public places, I would not pass the hallways when boys were there. I would no longer sit alone in a room with a boy or man.

This was how I grew up, allergic to men and the hurt they were wont to inflict.

I would give my number to every guy who asked, for fear of upsetting them into attempting to revenge or rape me.

Then in January 2017, I met him, believing my world was about to change — that the one who would wipe away my hurt and pain had arrived.

CHAPTER FOUR

THE EX

"I lost my virginity when I was fifteen, although lost is a funny word for it. I didn't misplace it like a homework assignment or a cell phone. It wasn't like I could find it again and tuck it back in there."
— Mindy Mejia

I have always been a hopeless romantic. As a teenager and young adult, I would read romance novels to get over a sad or gloomy mood and feed my fantasies of what my ideal man should look and act like. He had to be tall; he had to love and cherish me.

Memories of my abusive past would not let me consider myself a virgin; although, I had never had sex. I did not date through my university years. Aside from the fact that I had never felt any attraction towards men, I was a 'good' girl, whose ultimate desire was to graduate and date a precious man who would love, cherish, and marry me.

When I turned 21 and went for my NYSC — the mandatory National Youth Service Corps programme for Nigerian graduates — my former university roommate introduced me to Simi. He was tall and handsome; my dream man. I did not have relevant experience in that area, but I was excited to finally have a boyfriend. We would talk on phone and he would tell me he liked me and promise to give me a big kiss when we met.

Our first meeting was at a family Christmas party he invited me to. He kissed me like he promised. It was not a big kiss.

The second time we met, he had invited me to his house, which was in fact his father's house, for an outing later that day. The house was magnificent, with several self-contained quarters, each of which was allocated to Simi and his siblings.

In his room, I sat on the bed. We talked for a while, then we kissed. The kissing, this time, was great – like the authors of my numerous romantic novels had described. I could feel his growing penis push against my Baby Phat jeans. He started to pull them off but I asked him to stop.

'Nothing will happen,' he assured me. So, I helped him take my jeans off.

The passion was intense; my thoughts were colliding, and when he began to pull off my panties, I did not stop him. Then, he took off his boxers and lowered his penis inside me. It hurt more than I remember, so I pushed him off. He lowered himself to try a second time, pushing harder. The pain barged into me like a stranger in an unwanted place. I screamed and pushed him off again.

When I managed to sit up, I realised I was bleeding. It took a while to assimilate and accept the confirmation of my virginhood. Well, at least, I was a virgin, a while ago. Sorrow from unknown places within me pooled a well of tears in my eyes; Simi consoled me. He said he was surprised to find out I was a virgin.

'You are a virtuous woman, Seyi. I will marry you,' he said as he cradled me.

The pain felt lighter as I rested my head against his chest. But acceptance was difficult – I wanted my virginity back; I wanted a chance to lose it under better circumstances.

I soon found the courage to stop crying and leave for home – but the bleeding did not stop, several rolls of tissue paper and sanitary pads later. I was afraid I would die from losing my virginity.

Later that day, Simi called, admonishing me to use blood tonic and checking to be sure I was doing fine. It warmed my heart to know he cared, and that offered sufficient consolation for my loss – Simi was going to marry me.

We met a few times after then — sex was still painful and unpleasurable. On one of those encounters, I noticed Simi had saved my name on his phone as 'Seyi CU'. My heart skipped a beat; my future husband had saved my number with the wrong name. I was not sure how to confront the situation, so I did not.

The next time he asked to meet, it was over a chat. I replied his request, demanding that he took me on a proper date. He made excuses. I accused him of being a terrible boyfriend.

'Truth is, I only see you as a friend, Seyi,' he typed back.

I read the message and I started to shiver.

'Simi, you are a bastard,' I replied.

'I know,' he responded.

I came down with malaria immediately and hated Simi for the longest time. I promised myself to never let any man hurt me as much, again.

CHAPTER FIVE

THE MAN

"Sometimes you have to choose between being lonely and being crazy."
— Anonymous

Facebook is my family. My followers there know a lot about me. In 2016, I began posting stories about the challenges and joys of living with my kids, and people would comment and share their thoughts. I never really registered names.

On December 30, 2016, I was involved in a *marwa* accident. The tricycle, carrying me and other passengers, had fallen on its side and landed on my head. Onlookers and good Samaritans quickly gathered to pull out the passengers from the toppled tricycle and soon moved on to other things. No one saw me, until somebody yelled, '*Eni kan yi wan be!*' Someone is still in there!

After a few shoves and grunts, the troop of rescuers successfully raised the tricycle and helped me out, unscathed – except for the swelling on my head, which resulted from the pressure of the tricycle landing and resting on my head. I was, soon, accompanied to the hospital where I was advised to do a brain/ head scan, to rule out chances of any eventualities. Unfortunately, the nearest hospital did not run scans on Fridays, and sent me home with painkillers instead – asking that I return the next day for a thorough check. By nightfall, I was afraid I would die from a brain bleed before dawn. I had to inform my Facebook followers, just in case.

Shortly after my post, I received a private message from Toba Adelade, one of my Facebook 'friends', who was otherwise, a stranger. He said he was glad that I was okay and asked for my account details so he could send me some money. I sent him the organization's account number, but he insisted on having my personal account number instead.

'I know it can be a lonely road for people like you,' he said. 'So, it is you I want to give the money to. It's a personal gift.'

I am naturally wary of humans, so my first instinct was to check out his profile. I noticed we had mutual friends and that he was a member of the Covenant University Alumni Facebook group, which meant he was a CU graduate; we were leaves from the same branch. I let my guard down.

I sent him my GT Bank account number and he sent me ₦20, 000. I thanked him.

He asked if I had a nickname because he would like to make me a customized shirt and cap with my name on it. I was pleased with this person who saw me as a *person*. Finally, here was someone who realised that people like me, who gave their all to humanity, also needed help and attention.

'Sunkit,' I replied.

Then, he asked for my address. He said he would deliver the package himself, if he had some spare time. Otherwise, he would send a delivery man.

I gave him my address.

*

Sunday, January 8, 2017

Church service had just ended. I was heading towards the bus stop with my kids to enter a *marwa* when I got a call. It was Toba. He said he was at Eleshin bus stop, trying to locate my house so he could deliver the shirts. I gave him directions and told him I would join him shortly.

'I have to take an *okada* home. Someone is waiting,' I told my kids, as soon as I ended the call. I, then, gave them money to take a *marwa*, while I immediately took a bike home.

When I got there, he had parked his silver RAV4 SUV in front of our compound, waiting for me. I let him into the house, and opened the windows to let fresh air in.

'I like your jumpsuit,' he said.

'Thank you,' I replied, smiling. I was quite worried about being alone with a man, but I reminded myself that he was from CU – and CU graduates were respectable. At that exact moment, my kids burst in, much to my relief. They greeted him and went to their rooms, as we took our seats, facing each other.

We talked briefly about Covenant University before he gave me the cap and shirt he had originally come to deliver. The cap was blue, and the shirt, brown; his brand name and logo, passionately imprinted on the back of each. I thanked him. I hated the fabric of the shirt.

As soon as he left, I took pictures with the shirt and cap, sent them to him on WhatsApp with a thank you message, and put them away. We didn't speak again for a couple of weeks.

One afternoon, he sent me a message apologising for being MIA. He said he had been treating typhoid fever.

'It's fine,' I messaged back. 'I was ill too.'

We started to text more often.

I needed hoodies for my kids, so I contracted him to make them. He refused payment when he delivered the order.

By this time, I was aware of my growing feelings for this man who was nice to me and my kids, but I did not tell him about it. We continued our erratic conversations. Occasionally, he would ask how the kids were doing, and whether he could visit them; when he did, he would come bearing gifts. Some of my kids loved him, some did not and never came to; but they all loved his gifts.

I liked him, but he still lived with his parents, which was a major consideration for me. According to him, living alone meant people would visit him, uninvited; living with his parents meant less unwelcome guests.

I made a mental note that there could never be an 'us'.

*

Wednesday, April 19, 2017

We had been chatting on WhatsApp for close to four months, no major phone calls, when we started talking about past relationships. I told him how they literally had never worked for me, and he said the same too.

'All the girls I've ever dated did me dirty. I have decided to just be on my own.'

I said nothing; he sent another message.

'I wonder if our two broken hearts can come together and make each other happy.'

'We can give it a try,' I replied.

He thought I was joking, so, he called to confirm it.

'Yes, we can give it a try,' I affirmed.

And so, we began our relationship.

I was only partly committed, protecting my heart so that if it didn't work out, I could move on. I was not a fan of marriages either, so I did not see the relationship progressing beyond a lifelong partnership, if that worked out.

I secretly hoped that he would start working towards getting his own place as we worked on building the relationship. I was committed to helping him succeed as much as I could.

Toba was the picturesque romance novel dream man. He showered me with immense love and care — feelings so new and unusual to me, that I begged him to take it down a notch. He did not.

When I complained about a headache, he was right at my house in Ikorodu. He surprised me with meals I loved and constantly proclaimed how I had brought meaning to his life. He called me 'LaVida'.

'It means you are my life,' he had once said.

He made me T-shirts with LaVida written boldly on them, and I wore them with pride. I was sure I was in love. He offered me rides in his car. Whenever we had arguments, he was quick to apologise.

'I can't sleep if you're upset with me, *Regina Mei*.' He said it meant 'My Queen'.

His gestures were warm, thoughtful and plentiful, but I was still not ready to commit fully. When we had fights, it was always about me being busy or not replying to messages on time. I worried that he didn't have enough to do, which was why he found my being busy problematic, but I never said this to him. Instead, I would ask him to respect the fact that I was a busy person and promise to make time for him when the need arose.

'I know when you're online and when you have seen a message,' he would say, and a quarrel will ensue. 'If you don't love me, tell me,' he would conclude.

Then, I would reiterate for the umpteenth time, 'I do love you. I just do not have time to reply all messages.'

One afternoon, after a disagreement, he expressed his concern about my commitment to the relationship. I had wanted to blame his comment on his insecurities from past failed relationships but decided against it. I resolved that it was worth investing another 10% of my emotions in, and so, I did.

He asked about my past, but I refused to disclose the details – they were too unmade, unfair and un-healed to be shared. He insisted, offering to heal my hurt; so, I told him — despite how discomforting, revisiting them was. I felt some relief after sharing my story with him. He did not apologise for the other men, but he promised to never hurt me. I believed him.

Soon, I would trust him the way that I trusted only my dad and brothers. After all, I was his *LaVida*, his life.

His words were mostly the right choice, timely and comforting, that they made my heart soar. I began to believe he was the one man who would truly love me like I desired to be loved, the one who would make up for all the hurts and pains the other men had caused me.

*

The first time we spent the night together, he came to visit me at a writer's workshop I attended. His mother and sisters called him ceaselessly to ask of his whereabouts and why he was not back home yet. When he mentioned to them that he would not be returning home that night, they seemed upset. I found this very strange, but he assured me it only happened because he still lived with them.

He left the next morning.

The scenario was the same every other time we spent the night together – there was always a call from Mummy and Daddy.

I let him know that I felt like I was dating a teenager.

'I'm sorry, LaVida,' he apologised. 'I'm working on getting my own place soon and then, I'll be free from the monitoring.'

I was excited to hear that.

One day, he suggested that I meet his parents — they wanted to know the person he was always going to visit. 'My mum is worried that I'm with one of those terrible girls, the kind of characters they watch in Yoruba movies,' he said.

This was a huge step for me, but it looked like it would make him happy, so I obliged. His parents lived in a big duplex. His mum's expression, on seeing me, was that of amusement, despite the pleasing smile that lit up her face. It was as though she couldn't believe I existed and that someone had agreed to be with her son. His dad didn't say much.

During the 2017 Baddo incident at Ikorodu — a time when several seemingly random, brutal killings by a sinister group had people worried and afraid — he advised that I come and stay at his parent's until the insecurity subsided.

'You can return once things get back to normal,' he said.

I refused. I told him there was no way I was leaving my kids behind.

'You are putting the safety of these children over yours.'

'I am putting their safety on the same level as mine.'

'Look, you are like a football club to these kids. Once they are tired of you, they will leave.'

I hated that he said those words to me. 'My kids were in my life before you, and they will remain even if you choose to leave,' I said.

A few days later, he apologised. 'I just want to make sure you're safe, LaVida. You are always taking care of others, so I am here to take care of you.'

Those were the words that made everything right again.

I wanted to make our first Valentine's as a couple, special; it was my first valentine with a boyfriend. I was sure he wanted to make it a great day for us too. I messaged a jeweller to make me a bracelet with 'Sunshine' and 'You are my sunshine on a rainy day' engraved on either side of it. This gift cost me 80% of the money I had, and I was very excited to see what he got for me.

On Valentine's Day, I did not hear from him, so I messaged him to know what the plan was. There was no plan but there were countless excuses — of how he could not leave the house, and how the gifts he had bought could not be delivered to Ikorodu.

I was heartbroken. 'I had a gift prepared for you,' I said.

'I prepared a gift for you too, LaVida. It's not my fault that it couldn't be delivered.'

Days later, when we met, he visited empty-handed. When I gave him the bracelet I had customised for him, he said 'thank you' before needlessly lamenting about the fake quality of the jewellery.

It hurt, but I let it go.

I never got my Valentine's Day gift from him.

*

One afternoon, we went to eat out at Emperor, a roadside restaurant at Ikorodu. He was unusually quiet.

Eventually, he spoke. 'I want to tell you something.'

'Tell me. I'm all ears.'

He hesitated, then said, 'I am thinking of relocating to Canada.'

I was confused. 'What do you mean, you're thinking about it? You want to write the exam?'

'I've written the exam. I'm slated to go to Ghana for an interview.'

I was upset, but I did not know how to express it, so I kept mute.

'I love you so much, LaVida,' he said, taking my hands in his. 'You are my life. Even if I travel, we can still make it work. You can also start working on coming to join me in Canada, you know.'

As he continued to speak, I realised he had a full plan on how to start his clothing production business in Canada.

'I wish you good luck, Toba. Really, I do. But I have no plans of leaving Nigeria,' I told him, forthrightly. I had kids who looked up to me every day and I was not about to leave them alone.

He spent the days that followed convincing me to consider it. 'You can start by writing IELTS at least,' he would say.

It did not take long after then for me to start to *really* think about it. He brought me some past questions, and even as I looked through them, I was unsure. I knew I could not be fulfilled living somewhere else.

Days to his trip to Ghana for the Canadian interview, he asked me to go with him. I declined. 'Regina Mei, I really want you to come to Ghana with me,' he said, a few days later, when he visited my house.

'I can't pay for the trip, Toba.'

'You don't have to. I'm paying for everything, I promise.'

'I don't want to be a liability. I'm not comfortable with it.' This was something that bothered me a lot.

'LaVida, it's fine. I need you by my side for this big step.'

Eventually, I agreed to go with him.

On our first night in Ghana, he video-called a girl, asking where she lived. He told her his girlfriend was beside him.

The girl didn't believe him. 'You would not be calling me at this hour if your girlfriend were there.'

I told him when he ended the call, 'I feel highly insulted that you would video call a girl right here in my presence.'

'I'm sorry LaVida,' he apologised. 'I just wanted to show you off, so she can know I have someone better.'

His interview was the next morning, so I decided to let it go. Unfortunately, he returned with bad news; he didn't get in.

All my efforts to pacify him were met with cold shoulders. It was as though I wasn't there. He called his parents and sister to tell them about it, giving answers to the same questions he had refused to respond to when I asked him. His demeanour, later that night, as we lay in bed, was no different.

'Toba, I don't like the way you treat me sometimes,' I said.

'Maybe we should break up then.'

My heart shattered. 'What did you say?'

'Maybe we should break up,' he repeated.

I was in shock. I began to shiver. I sent Jessica a message: *'Toba just told me that he thinks we should break up!'*

'What? Leave where he is immediately. Go home.'

'I am with him in Ghana, on a trip he paid for.'

'SHIT! Okay, just try to calm down and stay calm.'

My eyes grew heavy with tears and they soon began to fall. I made to leave the room. He pulled me back.

'I was just joking and testing you.'

'This is the most ridiculous and insensitive joke I have ever had to experience! I am taking the breakup seriously.'

He continued to apologise, but I ignored him. After a while, he stepped out of the room. At this time, I had become feverish and started to run a temperature. When he came back about an hour later, I was under the duvet, still shivering.

'Are you still leaving me or not?' he asked. I did not respond.

He headed out to the balcony of the hotel room, and soon an unfamiliar smell wafted through the air. I stepped out to find him puffing on a cigarette. I did not know he smoked.

His behaviour became strange and erratic that I considered calling his mother.

'Smoking is not a way to get me to change my mind,' I told him.

Seeing that it was impossible to have a decent conversation with him, I decided it was best to leave him with his troubles. I furtively took a picture of the cigarette and went to sleep.

On our way to Nigeria the following morning, he was apologetic, but I had no plans of going back on my word. I sent a message to his mum, requesting to speak with her. She called me soon after, at which point I told her about the picture, which I had earlier sent to her. She said she was relieved it was not something worse. I went further to explain how things had played out during the trip. She asked me to be calm.

'He is probably stressed from the Canada thing,' she said, apologising on his behalf and begging me to listen to his pleas.

A week later, I took him back.

*

The first time he asked me for money was the night of my 26th birthday.

I was attending a writers' workshop at Best Western Hotel, and the day had been all shades of fun — cake, laughter, and banter, until his visit. My birthday is important to me, and having had the best day, I had looked forward to having the best night with my lover. But, on setting eyes on him, the shock I was to receive much later became imminent.

He had bought me a perfume that I wanted, but he did not present it to me. Instead, he left it on a table and sat by himself on the lone chair in the room, looking forlorn.

His sadness saddened me. After several unsuccessful attempts at finding out what the problem was, while lying in bed, he revealed that he had something to show me.

'Okay,' I responded, cautiously.

'This is a treasury bill,' he said, pointing to a document on his phone.

I could see that there was about four million naira in it.

'This is money I have saved,' he continued.

I had very little interest in the conversation. I don't like to know about other people's money, and I don't like to disclose details about my money to other people.

He said he needed to do a clothing deal, and he had to pay some money, but he couldn't liquidate his treasury bills investment yet.

'Please, I need you to lend me some money,' he begged. 'I will pay back next week.'

I was wary. Lending a man money was something I was certain I would never do, something I always told myself I would never do. However, this was not 'a man', he was *the man* I loved — nice, from a good family that seemed to have it all together, and a person of integrity as far as I could tell. I reckoned he would pay back.

The money he asked for was literally all I had, so I made him promise to return it.

'I promise I will pay you back next week, LaVida. Please.'

I lent him the money, and true to his word, he returned it the week after.

That was not the last time he would borrow money from me, but it was one of the few occasions he paid back like he said he would.

He would borrow money ceaselessly — to fix his car, which always looked the same; to upgrade his shop, which he never used; to push several business deals that never saw the light of day — most of which he never paid back.

Each time I asked him about the loans, he would cry and accuse me of disrespecting him. It always hurt that he hurt, so I would wind up consoling him. I was blinded by love.

And each time we had arguments during our courtship, he would say, 'I am not with you for your money.' I would laugh and respond, 'I do not have enough money for someone to want to be with me because of it.'

I was confident that, of the many reasons why we chose to date, financial manipulation was not one. We were both hard workers. He had dreams of building a multi-generational empire, at the core of which stood his strong and famous clothing brand; I had dreams of building a legacy. I had hoped we could work together to

build on those dreams, but the dreams were not aligning
– hope was failing.

*

I loved to buy him gifts, to express my affection. Today, it was Nike slides; tomorrow, a book. His eyes would light up on each occasion and we would make love, so passionate it made time stand still. I relished the feeling and was committed to reliving it every way that I could.

But the money problems were a persistent thorn in the flesh of our budding relationship.

One day, when he complained about not having money, I asked about his clothing clients. He said the friend for whom he customised socks was only using him and hardly paid.

'He doesn't even let me post the work I do for him on social media!' He lamented.

'Why not sign a deal with him and collect your money? I think you should do that.'

He agreed to do this. Days later, he announced that their business relationship had ended.

Shortly after then, he complained that business opportunities no longer came like they used to. Being a novice to his line of business, I had no words of advice, but I urged him not to give up.

'I think you're angry with me and that's why things are not working for me,' he said.

I was taken aback.

'Pray for me, LaVida.'

I prayed for him. Then, I started to tell everyone I knew about his customised t-shirts and successfully introduced him to a few new customers.

During some of his subsequent visits, he brought food, which he said he bought with money from jobs done for those new customers – perhaps, a commission for my goodwill or an attestation to his ability to make nice gestures when he had the means. But I wanted to go on dates, with him.

When I suggested it, his excuse was same: he had no money.

Then, I would say, 'Poor teenagers still find a way to go on dates with each other. We can find something.' And we would fight.

We never went on dates.

*

It was too late by the time I realised he had alienated me from my loved ones and support system, without my being conscious of it.

First, he decided my therapist was unimportant. 'I am a therapist too. All my friends call me to talk to me. You can also talk to me,' he said.

So, I stopped calling my therapist and started telling him everything. When I had a fight with my family and left the house with suicide on my mind, he was the first person I called. I needed to be anywhere but home, at my parent's. He provided succour.

67

He offered that I come to his parent's, but I preferred to be in a neutral environment, so we lodged in a hotel together. I paid for the space, he gave me a shoulder to cry on and a listening ear — it was a noble bargain.

He said that life was meaningless, and he would rather we died together when I was ready. It was a homophilic moment — the closest I had ever felt to being understood by anyone.

It was not long before I stopped talking to anyone but him — even Jessica.

*

I noticed his strong aversion to rape. He would often talk about how rapists should be killed and a couple of times, he talked about how women sometimes accused men falsely.

One afternoon, he told me the story of his promiscuous twin sisters-in-law. He said they hardly had reasons to speak, except on such occasions that the sisters asked him to help them set up their phones. On one of such days, he said he stumbled upon a message that revealed that one of the girls was planning to have an abortion. According to him, when she noticed he had found out her secret, she announced to all occupants in the house that he had raped her. It was an upsetting incident for him, he acquiesced, but what was more upsetting was the fact that his father did not believe him.

'How could I have raped her in a house so big and no one would hear?' he asked me, incredulously, as if my opinion mattered.

He continued, saying he had made up his mind to leave his parent's house after that incident, until his mum appealed to him to reconsider.

'I never raped this girl, LaVida. She lied against me,' he told me.

I believed him. I hated this girl for lying against him — for spitting in the faces of real rape victims.

*

But there would be many more stories, of many other girls. 'I have something to tell you,' he said, one afternoon, with a very worried look on his face. He had come to visit me.

'Okay, tell me. I'm all ears.'

'It's about Lola.'

Lola was a member of the Nehemiah group at our church, Daystar Christian Centre.

'What about Lola?'

'She has been stalking me and trying to get me to ask her out. I have done all I can to keep her away from me, but she keeps coming back. I have reported her to my unit director, to ask her to please stop following and stalking me.'

'Wow.'

'She even goes as far as saying 'I must marry you' and that's really alarming. She is the reason I have decided I won't be attending Nehemiah meetings anymore.'

'Hmm. Please be very careful,' I told him.

Another day, it was how his ex-girlfriend broke his heart. 'I was in another country and I called her. She sounded very exhausted, so I asked her if she was having sex. She said yes. I ended the call immediately and never dated anyone again after that. That experience made me give up on relationships and marriage.'

'I'm so sorry you had to go through that.' I said.

'You are the one who has renewed my hope in love and relationships, Regina Mei.'

I felt special.

Soon, he would tell me about the girl in Aberdeen who liked him so much that she went to his apartment and slept beside him naked, just so he could have sex with her.

'The thing is, I have very strong self-control. I didn't do anything with her at all. The next morning, I kissed her and apologised to her for not having sex with her. She was crying as she left.'

'You have way too many stories with women. And you're the superhero in every story. Ah! I'm beginning to think some of them are lies,' I told him.

He laughed. 'You don't have to believe me but it is the truth.'

I did not believe him this time, but I didn't argue.

*

Sometimes, I asked myself whether I was suffering from memory loss. He would say something, and I would hear him say it, but he would deny it soon after. He would retell stories, incidents, events in such a way that I would forget what he had originally said, or how I responded. It was a mass of mess.

I began to allude my forgetfulness to my busy lifestyle. Why else was I suddenly be unable to remember what was said?

He agreed. 'You do not pay attention. That is why.' I believed him.

He would randomly ask about us getting married. I did not believe in marriages. I would say, 'Marriage changes everything. I am worried you will change.' And he would respond, saying, 'I am the same man, LaVida. We already have sex like a married couple, and we do a lot together.'

Then I would say, 'I'm not ready. And you need to at least leave your parent's house and rent your own place first.'

That was before I began to experience immense pressure from my family. Before my ultimate desire was to move out of my family home, so I could have some space and independence and be closer to town so my kids could go for events. When this happened, I started to shop for houses in Magodo. But for every house I found, Toba would present himself as my husband, because Lagos Landlords would not rent houses to single women.

One of the agents we encountered had more questions than we expected. So much so, we elevated our act and made up a wedding date to satisfy the property's assigned lawyer. The lawyer advised me not to do a registry wedding. He said it put women at a disadvantage.

'I am a lawyer, and I will never let my daughter do a registry wedding,' he emphasised.

I nodded, absentmindedly; I knew we were not getting married.

Until one day, when I found myself asking him, 'What if we do get married?'

'Are you serious' he asked.

'Yes, I'm serious.'

The more I thought about it, the more obvious it seemed that marriage would be a perfect way to overcome the pressure I was facing on the family front about everything from my choice of church, to what I did with my time. I decided that marriage couldn't be so bad.

And, so began the marriage preparations.

I told Gbemi, with whom I had been friends since our university days, about the wedding plans. She was worried at how sudden it was. 'Are you sure you want to do this?'

'Yes. I am sure I want to do this.'

Jessica was more worried when she heard.

'Are you not just doing this because he accepts your kids?'

'No, that's not it,' I said, even though deep down, I knew she was right.

I was conscious of the fact that I had considered breaking up with him many times in the past, but decided against it because I was afraid of being lonely, afraid that no other man would love me the way he did, afraid that no man would want to be with a lady who housed 10 children.

I wanted an escape.

'Please, Seyi, think about this very well. Marriage is not a bed of roses, and this guy seems quite controlling and possessive. Please, I'm begging you, take your time and think this through.'

'I've thought it through, Jessica. I have. Thank you so much for your care and concern. I am very sure about this.'

'Okay,' she said, leaning over to hug me. 'I wish you well.'

CHAPTER SIX

AFTER I SAY 'I DO'

"Soul Abuse is the destruction of a victim's awareness of the strength within their soul. It stems from the abuser's intention to corrupt another's understanding of their own significance."
— Lorraine Nilon

We got married on my 27th birthday.

The day before our wedding, we had argued about bride prices and the goat that my parents insisted must be a part of the ceremony. His family did not want to have to travel with a goat, so I agreed to get someone to buy the goat once they sent the money. As soon as I received the money, I gave it to my brother-in-law, who helped us buy the goat. All my fiancé (at the time) had to do was pick it up.

He was displeased with my request. He misconstrued my words and made me question myself; I was not sure I wanted to marry him the next day. But who could I tell a day before my wedding that I no longer wanted to be married?

On Thursday, October 4, 2018, I put on my white dress, ready for the registry. He called me; he sounded sweet. I was still unsure about my decision, but I knew there was no going back.

I put on a smile.

I can do this.

We had a quiet ceremony at the registry and at my parent's house, where we held the engagement ceremony. I was excited about what would follow, and curious to know what he had bought me for my birthday.

After the ceremony, we drove his parents back home, where his mother poured a bowl of water on my feet and said a prayer, before I was let in. The water felt cold against my feet and the tradition was alien to me but I trusted them, and I trusted her, so I said amen to her prayers.

We headed upstairs and into his room to pick some of his things. His mother soon came in, surprised to see us packing.

'*Mo ro boya e ma duro sibi lale yi ni?*' she said, her face soft and smiling as always. *I thought you'd stay here tonight.*

I chuckled, thinking it was a joke. I realised it wasn't when she lingered for a response. My husband did not give one, so I did. '*Rara ma.*' She nodded, still smiling, and left the room.

As we drove off to Magodo from his parent's, I asked him the question I had been curious to get answers to all day.

'So when will I get my birthday gift?'

He smiled. 'I didn't get you anything.'

I laughed it off at first, certain he was joking.

'I'm sorry. I just couldn't decide what to get you. Plus, I don't have any money on me.'

He was not joking. 'Even if it was a mug, Toba. Anything but nothing. I would have appreciated it.'

He flashed the smile he used to diffuse situations. The one that said, *let's not make a big deal about this.* 'I'm sorry. I'll make it up to you once I have money.'

I nodded, helplessly. But I was deeply hurt that the man I married did not consider me important enough to get me a birthday gift. Even if it were sand wrapped in a paper. Anything but nothing. It was our first day being married and I was unhappy.

But the wedding night sex was good — so good, it almost absolved his earlier misdeeds. I was grateful that the kids were not around.

*

His sister made me a big cake to celebrate my birthday – even though my *own* husband didn't find me worthy of a gift. I was overwhelmed and grateful.

Not long after we got married, his brother gifted us a big-screen TV. Soon after this, his sister gifted us a water dispenser.

I was so impressed by how nice his family was, and I mentioned this to him. 'It's almost like they'd go the extra mile for you,' I teased.

By the time I found out the car he had been driving was bought by his sister, and assigned exclusively for his use, I was almost certain his family was perfect.

'Make sure you don't tell them anything about us,' he said. 'My family members don't share personal details with each other.'

I thought it was weird, but I shrugged my sentiments off, assuming it was nothing but a family dynamic that made them so close-knit.

Whenever he had to take a call from any of his siblings or parents, he would leave the room, to return when the call was over. I never heard their conversations, but this did not bother me.

When his sister had a baby, he did not tell me. I overheard it during one of his private calls but feigned ignorance, hoping to hear it from him. When he told me two days later, I confronted him about not telling me earlier.

'I was asked not to tell anyone,' he said.

'Am I anyone?'

He did not respond.

I decided to let things be.

*

His birthday was 11 days after mine. I bought him a couple of shorts. When I presented them to him, his countenance was worrisome.

'Thank you,' he said, but it did not reach his eyes.

Then, we argued about something I can no longer remember. That was before he left the house and refused to take my calls until he returned about two hours later, with a box of pizza and ice cream.

'This is how I want to celebrate my birthday with the kids,' he said.

I did not eat out of the pizza.

The next morning, he returned the birthday gift. 'Since you did not eat the pizza I got, I don't want your gift.'

I accepted my gift back and returned the wedding ring to him. 'I do not want to be married to you anyways,' I said, defiantly.

This infuriated him. 'I am going to have to call your mum to let her know what you have done!'

'Don't even try it, Toba. I'm warning you. My business is my business!'

As I tried to get the phone from him, I saw that he had started dialling a number, and it was his mum's, not mine.

'End that call, Toba.'

'It's your fault that I accidentally dialled your mum.' He said, holding his phone out of my reach.

'You are calling YOUR mother!' I argued.

'I am calling your mother, not mine,' he countered, seemingly confused. For a moment, I thought I saw it wrong.

But when he put the phone to his ear, and started to speak — immediately apologising to his mother for calling accidentally, and going right ahead to tell her about how I returned his ring, I realised his intention all along had been to call his mother. His words were inconsistent with his actions.

His mother soon asked to speak with me. 'Calm down,' she said, when I took the phone and greeted her.

I explained to her that I did not appreciate the fact that my husband was bringing a third party into our relationship. She went silent for a beat, and then continued to speak.

'Please take your ring back, my dear. It is too early for fights like this. You need to be patient, you hear?'

I thanked her and ended the call. But the argument continued, until it left me exhausted and crying.

'I feel like you disrespect me because of money I have borrowed from you,' he said.

I promptly put my pain aside and comforted him. 'I would never disrespect you because of that. Never.'

'I assure you, I will pay back everything I owe you.'

'Thank you. Please let's talk about something else.'

We did not have make up sex; I was on my period.

*

After the wedding, my name remained Seyi Oluyole. We had discussed about name change a long time before the wedding and agreed that I would be keeping my name.

We had no plans of having a baby within the first year; it was also something we discussed before the marriage. This was especially important because his finances needed to get better. I was not ready to birth a child into struggle and poverty. Neither was I about to start calling family members to beg for money for diapers and food. We both agreed that when finances got better, we could try for a child. This did not stop him from randomly hinting at getting me pregnant, at which point I would remind him that a child comes with huge responsibilities and financial strain.

*

We had been married for two months. Some days it was great, other days it wasn't. Yet, I never discussed my pain with anyone.

I had never gone through his phone — not even while we were dating — but on this particular night, something pushed me to. So, I picked up his phone, typed in the password and started to browse through.

There were a lot of deleted messages.

I visited his Twitter DM and saw an attempt at sexting; the lady had shut him down. Then, I saw a conversation with another lady where he was apologising, but I couldn't see why. Previous messages had been deleted. At this point, I had started to shiver.

His betrayal was glaring — this man, whom I had trusted with my entire heart; this man, who told me how he had never loved anyone the way he loved me. I didn't have the patience to go through his other phone or any other messages. I woke him up and asked him to tell me about the conversation I had just seen. He accused me of snooping through his phone.

'I want answers,' I insisted.

'I haven't spoken to any lady since we got married. That conversation was while we were dating. I wasn't sure you were fully into the relationship at the time. It was a time we were having issues.'

'These are all excuses!' I said, shivering and crying. My heart, broken afresh.

Then, his approach changed — from defensiveness to offering promises, to reminding me of the extenuating circumstances under which the events had occurred. 'It was a mistake, LaVida.'

I wondered about all the other women he might be involved with and this messed with my head for days. Through this, his attempts at re-assuring me that the events occurred during a temporary lapse of judgment continued. They were futile.

A few days later, he told me he had deleted his social media accounts.

'This is extreme,' I said.

He blamed social media for our issues, but I cut him off. 'You started speaking to this girl on your own, remember?'

He insisted his being off social media was the best thing for our relationship, although I expressed worry about his business visibility and marketing, which would suffer from his social media absence.

News flash: he lied — he never deleted them. I would find out later that he had a secret account, where he continued to propagate his other agendas. It was amusing, because he really didn't need to delete social media or lie that he did.

*

As a married couple, it was my desire that my other half would be as successful as I was, and I considered it my duty to help him climb the ladder of success. I suggested ideas for his clothing and printing business and offered him my platform for marketing purposes.

'You can sell your merchandise through my academy,' I suggested.

He agreed, in principle but not in action — he made no moves to implement my suggestions.

But he helped with my kids, especially by making his car available for our numerous trips. I would want to hire a car or van, and he'd offer to give us a ride. Although it was cramped, it was cheaper; the kids and I were grateful for this.

Each time we got back home and alighted from his car, he would complain that the kids got his car dirty. So, I would ask them to clean the car and thank him for the kind gesture. He would tell them not to bother, suggesting that it pleased him to be of assistance, yet he would complain after every trip.

One day, he asked me, 'What do I gain from doing this?' He went on to complain about how he had been spending time, working on my project, but had nothing to show for it.

'Toba, whenever you feel like the pressure of volunteering is too much, just stop, please,' I offered, empathetically. 'You don't have to go all out of your way.'

He insisted that he wanted to help but emphasized his need to feel rewarded.

'We can hire you as a business manager, since you have great ideas,' I said.

He agreed.

When we prepared a contract of engagement, he persistently refused to sign. He was upset that I would ask him to sign a contract. 'I'm your husband!' He lamented.

'This is a job. You need to sign a document,' I would remind him, each time the conversation ensued.

Soon, he was demanding to be a business partner.

This did not feel right, but he was my husband. I didn't want to say no. I didn't want to start a fight. So, I agreed, but made it clear we needed to sign a document.

He got upset again. 'I don't want to sign anything.'

'But you need to. This is business and it's important.'

'So, you don't trust me! Look, I'm not trying to steal your vision or your organization. I just want to support you.'

'I understand. You just need to sign a document, so we know our roles.'

After unsuccessful attempts at manipulating me into giving away my sweat on a platter of gold, he agreed to sign the document. I sent a message to my lawyer asking him to draft an agreement making me and my husband business partners.

My lawyer did not agree to this. 'I know how many years you have been working alone on your project for. No one can come from nowhere to become an equal partner.' So, he drafted a non-partnership agreement, which I emailed to my husband.

He was upset all over again.

I remember one argument, in particular. We were in the car, on Adeola Odeku Street, Victoria Island.

'That document reads like an employment. I don't want to be employed. I want to be a partner. The responsibilities are too much,' he complained.

'But you have to do some work at least,' I argued.

It was tiresome – the back and forth, so I asked my lawyer to redraft. He was adamant.

'Seyi, remember that I have your best interest at heart.'

'I know.' I was exhausted.

My lawyer insisted on leaving the agreement as it was; my husband refused to sign it, although he was already being referred to as the business manager and received a monthly allowance for that role.

I insisted that he sign the contract.

One day, he agreed to sign the document — on the grounds that his responsibilities were reviewed; he had cancelled out nearly all the responsibilities assigned to his role. I was appalled, and this led to another argument.

'You know what?' he said after a particularly heated episode, 'I will have to stop working for the academy.'

'That's okay,' I said, calmly.

He stared at me; surprise etched on his face. Then, he walked out, got in his car and drove off. I decided to rest, but he was back in no time.

'LaVida, I think it's best we work together. I know you will need me on a lot of assignments, and I won't want to turn you down.'

'Yes, it's best. As soon as you sign the document, we can make progress.' That was where the conversation died.

Then, he wanted us to open a joint account, where we would both put in a percentage of our earnings. I knew this was a stupid move — for me, and that it would be a wrong decision to make, but I agreed. I agreed because I trusted him, and believed he wanted the best for me and our union. We never opened the account, and in retrospect, I am eternally thankful for this.

*

I was putting a lot of effort into the growth of my organisation and academy, and I needed a mentor to support the process, so I reached out to one of the women I revered and thought fit for the role. She asked me to send her a sustainable one-year plan and budget with goals. I was excited about this; the fact that she responded at all, thrilled me the most.

I got to work immediately, and of course, sought the collaboration of my business manager — who had the fortunes of being my husband, which led to another fight. As he had boldly declared several times in the past, he was not interested in doing the work that came with the role. At this point, I was tired and upset. How could I grow if this man would not pull his own weight?

Soon, my anger peaked, and I moved out of our matrimonial room into the spare room. Within a few hours of being in the spare room, I realised that I could think better and stay focused on tasks. It was as though a fog had cleared and I was in a better place mentally.

After spending a night in the spare room, he asked me back to our room. I declined. We had settled our differences, but I felt more comfortable in the spare room.

The spare room was right beside our matrimonial room, but its door was faulty, so it was always slightly open. One night, a noise woke me from my sleep and pried my eyes open — my husband was sneaking out of our room. He was gone for a few minutes, and then he was back. I found this funny, and so, I overlooked it.

I continued to sleep and work in the spare room and would only go to the other room to get some of my belongings or be with him, on the rare occasions that he asked. I would notice Blessing spying on me in the spare room; sometimes at night, and sometimes in the early mornings, which I found strange. But I did not connect the dots.

One morning, she asked, 'Ma, why are you not sleeping in the other room?'

'I like it here,' I responded, smiling. Unsuspecting.

The night I decided to move back into the bedroom I shared with Toba was the night I found out what had been going on.

*

One afternoon, I woke up from a nap and checked my email notifications. There was an inbox from my boss, announcing that we had lost a colleague, who was also a friend to me. At first, I didn't understand. It was surreal. It took a couple of reads to assimilate the gravity of the email – *O* was gone. I screamed and burst into tears. Then, I ran downstairs; Toba was in the kitchen.

'*O* is dead,' I said.

He looked confused, so I reminded him that he had sold a shirt to *O* a year ago.

'Oh,' he said, hugging me briefly. 'That's how life is.' Before returning to what I met him doing.

The ache in my heart deepened. I wanted to mourn my friend and talk about him. He didn't want to hear it.

He did not even want to attend his memorial service, which was fine; until he changed his mind on the D-day, after I had dressed up and started to search for an Uber ride.

'I'll take you,' he said.

'Okay, thank you.' At least that meant I wouldn't have to spend time finding another Uber rider to take me back home.

We arrived in good time.

The moment I entered the room, my eyes fell on Jessica. From her tight smile, I could see the pain of loss. As we hugged each other, she whispered in my ear, 'You've lost weight.'

I had barely sat down for the service to begin when Toba said, 'We need to leave soon.'

I wanted to stay longer, but I knew it would turn into an argument that I didn't want. I had missed all these friends I used to hang out with before I got married, and now needed permission to do anything. I stood up to say a few words about *O*, the last time I saw him was at a workshop where he had shown me his genius.

It hurt to leave before I was ready to. I still often feel like I did not mourn *O* as I would have loved to, as he deserved. We lost him, and I did not get a chance to linger in his beautiful memory.

*

His more life-threatening tendencies started to manifest one afternoon. I was seated downstairs with the kids, on the couch under the staircase. I would often sit there while we played and made small talk. Toba came out from our room and addressed us from the top of the staircase. He was holding the padlock to the house gate.

'Come and take the padlock.'

I looked up at him. 'Throw it na,' I joked.

He didn't respond. I turned back to my kids, then *BOOM!*

That was the sound of the padlock landing right beside me on the couch — barely missing my head.

'Ah!' some of the children shouted.

I looked up at him in shock.

'You said I should throw it,' he said, unapologetically.

I thought it was a joke, it had to be.

Until something similar happened again.

We were having an argument about my foster kids being in my life, about him feeling like I did not appreciate him enough — although, I had lent him all my money, created a position for him at my organisation, and was even in the process of adding him to our board.

He always had something to complain about.

On this day, we were talking over each other. He was talking about the kids and I was also trying to make a point. He wanted me to be quiet and listen to him, but I wasn't going to let him take my voice, so I insisted on speaking. It annoyed him that I wouldn't shut up, so he grabbed me by my shoulders and shook me vigorously.

'Stop! It hurts!' I screamed.

He didn't stop. He shook me until I went quiet. Then, he let me go.

'I am sorry. I just needed you to shut up,' he said.

*

I had become a shadow of myself, someone who no longer knew who she was. Somehow, the union had made me lose my core and sense of self. To my kids, I had become a stranger; I would yell, scold and punish them more. They missed their Aunty Seyi; I missed my self too.

'You are too light-handed. You are spoiling them,' he would say to me.

And I always listened, because he said he only wanted the best for me. Until I began to feel the disconnection between me and my kids. I began to hear them speak amongst themselves about how they didn't want to be with me anymore. The turn of events was devastating but I didn't know what to do.

Whenever I complained to him, he would say, 'They are only a business tool.'

'No. they are my kids and I love them.'

'Of course. It's them you love, not me'

'But they were in my life before you. You met them in my life.'

And then we'd start fighting and eventually, I would agree with him.

Sarah, one of my kids, was having difficulties adjusting — she was naughty. She was only 6 years old when I met her. She'd steal at school and refuse to do her homework and morning duties. I was ready to be patient with her but he wanted her to leave. I tried to explain to him that all she needed was time, but he was adamant.

'It is either she leaves or I leave.'

I remember he was sitting on the bed in the room upstairs when he said this, and I was lost for words.

'You're being unfair, Toba.'

Still, I chose him, eventually.

*

Our sex life took a downward turn after the wedding night — first, it dwindled, until it became terrible. The duration became shorter, and the frequency reduced. Then, it became a gift he'd give me when I calmed down after an argument. As time went on, I lost the privilege to receive the gift, and it became something we did whenever he wanted it. I became too afraid and shy to ask for it because I was tired of being turned down. I eventually stopped asking and let him have me whenever he wanted.

I remember vividly, the night I took a shower, got dressed in blue lingerie and laid on the bed, looking sexy. He was not around, and I wanted to surprise him when he returned. While waiting, I dozed off. I woke up when he came in. He saw me in the lingerie and did not spare another look, before turning to other things. I don't remember ever feeling so dirty and unwanted.

One afternoon, he made me write and sign a note stating that he could have sex with me whenever he wanted, and that he could penetrate me even in my sleep. I wrote and signed the note. I wanted him to love me. To want me. I didn't mind whether it was while I was deep in sleep — so long as he wanted and loved me.

In the middle of the night, he'd turn me around and penetrate me. I can't count how often I'd wake up to him inside me, oil all over my vagina.

I began to feel like a sex slave. I would tell myself, 'Maybe I am a sex slave. Maybe that's my purpose on earth.' And I became content with that purpose. I justified all his actions that made me feel small. Because, he, at least, liked me for me. I told myself I was undeserving, and I must appreciate this man who loved me. And who knew? Maybe no one else would love me like he did.

He'd always say to me, 'You are troublesome.' And, so, I became grateful that he was able to accommodate my troubles. No other man would do that, I told myself.

*

One afternoon, I got a call from a guy I worked with. I had made his job easier by providing certain documents that he needed.

Excitedly, he said to me, 'I owe you lunch.' Then, he quickly backtracked.

'Is your business manager also your partner?'

'Yes. He is,' I responded.

'Oh okay. There's no need for lunch. But thank you for the help.'

When the call ended, I started to wonder if this person really liked me. Like, did he like me enough to want to date me?

I think there was a little shift in my brain from that day. I was awed by the fact that someone else could like me and find me desirable; that a successful man with a job, who wouldn't need to depend on me could *actually* like me.

Sometimes in the shower, I would wonder what life I could have with this other man. Would my life be less painful? Would he buy me any gifts? I was sure he had his own money and would not spend and finish mine; and that alone was enough.

Right in the middle of these thoughts, I would chastise myself, reminding myself to be grateful that someone was staying with me. I would tell myself that I had a husband who accepted all my faults and made me hot water to bathe on some mornings. I had no guarantee someone else would love me or care for me enough to make me hot water to bathe.

At this point in my life, I was terribly lacking in self-confidence.

I started to write on mirrors.

I am beautiful.

I deserve love.

I read these affirmations, but I no longer believed them.

It was him I believed — what he said, and what he did not say; what he did and what he did not do. I stopped wearing make-up because he said I was prettier without it.

When he stopped telling me he loved me, I was scared. I could not bear to lose this love that I had found, from this man generous enough to love me when no one else dared. I would complain about this often, but he would dismiss my concerns.

So, I devised ways to assure myself of his love. Like when he'd bring me hot water to bathe. Or the times when he'd cut up bananas in a cup of yoghurt for me. He seldom did these things, but the days he did, I felt so loved.

*

He had bad breath; he always did, and probably still does. Sometimes, it stank like a dead body. When he opened his mouth, I would quickly turn away. I used to offer him gum, while we were dating, hoping he'd get the hint. He never did.

Don't ask why I stayed. I don't know. I felt like I needed someone; he was there.

One day, I sent him a text about his bad breath. He told me he had a bad tooth which had decayed, and he'd usually clean it with cotton swabs so it wouldn't stink. I encouraged him to keep doing that.

When we got married, he stopped kissing me. I wanted him to kiss me, so I'd try to initiate it, but every trial met with his refusal. I wondered why.

One afternoon, I said, 'We barely kiss anymore.'

'It's because you no longer take care of yourself. Sometimes your mouth smells,' he said.

I was shocked to hear this — I brushed twice daily, I saw a dentist every six months, and I had never had halitosis (at least, I was not aware that I did). Could it be that people were too scared to tell me?

I smelt my breath that day and it seemed normal. I did not realise that he was projecting his problems on me. The next time I visited a supermarket, I bought Mentos gum and some minty sweets, and would always have them in my mouth. I hoped my breath would smell good enough and my husband with the decayed tooth and bad breath would want to smell it — and kiss me. Nothing changed.

Soon, he stopped telling me I was beautiful. Whenever a stranger complimented my beauty in his presence, his face would go dark. And when I complained that he didn't compliment me, he'd say he was stressed and didn't notice the way I looked.

Still, I wanted to make him happy. I wanted him to make sweet love to me, like he used to when we first started dating. I thought long and hard about what I could do for him. Then, I remembered his phone was faulty and he had been complaining about it for a while. Jackpot!

I bought him a new phone, hoping for his love and acknowledgement in return.

I got a kiss.

*

Whenever I caught him staring at a lady whom I also found pretty, I would say, 'I saw you,' hoping to make a joke out of it.

'You didn't catch anything,' he would say. 'Have you forgotten how scared of women I am? I was just looking at her as all these runs girls.'

Then, he'd proceed to recount the stories of how his friends would tease him about not being a real man because he was scared of women.

One day, I was paying for our items at The Prince supermarket, when his phone rang. I saw the picture of a woman across the screen just as he answered the phone. His answers were monosyllabic, and when he ended the call, I waited for him to tell me who the caller was. He didn't.

When we got back home, I asked him about the call. He said it was an old friend whom he never talked to, and that she'd called to ask if he was at home. 'I told her no.'

I was confused.

'She was asking if I'm at Okota.'

Okota? His father's house? His answers were not adding up but before I could say more, he asked, 'Do you think you are insecure?'

I shrugged. 'Maybe. I just wanted to know who the caller was. I saw a lady's picture.'

'It's nothing. I would never cheat on you. You know Junior only rises for you.'

I smiled. I foolishly believed him.

*

The first time I noticed that I had started to second-guess myself, my words and my confidence, was on the night before my TedXLagos talk in 2018. We were at the Muson Centre rehearsing my speech and the kids' dance presentation. We were not married at this time, but we had talked about getting married.

When we stepped out of the hall for a short break, he scolded me about something I had said while rehearsing my speech, and the way I said it.

'You only have negative things to say. You can't even say well done,' I complained, deeply hurt.

'You know I never want to hurt you,' he responded. 'I am only trying to help you.'

He would repeat those words to me a thousand times more, after criticizing how I did in an interview, the way I acted at a meeting, or the way I answered a professional call.

I started to doubt my words and proficiency. Every time I wanted to speak to someone, I would make him speak on my behalf or ask him what the right thing to say was. I stopped getting offended at the fact that I couldn't seem to do anything right in his eyes. Instead, I would replay his voice in my head, saying, *'you know I never want to hurt you.'* Those words became my succour, for every time he hurt or embarrassed me in public.

Slowly, he crushed my soul — so much so, that I couldn't think of a life without him. I didn't have the confidence to leave him because I thought no one else would want me and love me the way he loved me, with all my flaws. My life was so immersed in his that I felt like I would amount to nothing without him.

*

On some days, I rebelled against him.

I can't remember when I stopped wearing my wedding ring. I pulled it off once because it got itchy and had etched a mark on my finger. After I took it off, I remember feeling like I had lifted a heavy weight off myself. I didn't want to wear it anymore.

Taking off the ring also helped me realise I didn't want to be married anymore. The relationship was volatile; I was happy for a day and sad for the next three weeks. I was pulling so much emotional and financial weight, alone.

'That's how you stopped wearing your wedding ring,' he noted, once, while we were in the car.

'It makes my finger itch,' I told him.

'It's fine if you don't want to wear it.'

I stopped wearing it.

One afternoon, right after one of my features had aired on a TV station, he got on a call with his elder sister.

A few minutes after he had ended the call, he turned to ask, 'What do you think about a compound name? Oluyole – Adelade.

'We already had this conversation before we got married. My name is a brand and I am not changing it.'

Then, he complained about my shorts one evening, unprovoked, 'Don't you think your shorts are too short?'

I wore shorts a lot – before and after we got married – to the supermarket, around the estate, or to make dance videos and it had never been a subject of discourse.

'I have been wearing shorts since forever,' I responded, defiantly.

'Yes, but they seem too short.'

'They are fine. I like my shorts like this.'
We never discussed those things again.

*

I have small breasts. He made jokes about them a lot. We'd be laying on the bed and he'd say something like, 'There's no difference between your chest and mine.'

I would laugh, pretending it was funny.

I began to research ways to make my breasts bigger, and the effects of breast enlargement products and procedures.

After one of his jokes about my breasts, I asked him, 'Do you think my breasts are too small? Should I do an enlargement?'

He laughed and said, 'They are fine.'

I wished he had said, 'they are sexy' or something nicer.

Wishes aren't horses.

*

Our front door was an iron door, and it had been faulty since we moved in. One of the hinges that held the door had fallen out and so it had just one hinge holding it. We always went in and out through the back door and only opened the front door when we had visitors. It would take about two or three people to push it open.

One afternoon, Blessing tried to open the door without help. Of course, it was a bad idea — she didn't have enough strength to hold the door, so the bottom part hit her big toe. She didn't tell me when it happened. I found out from him, instead. It was rather strange to me that he was the one informing me about Blessing's injury.

I went to her, asking to take a look at the toe. Her big toenail had cracked.

'Let me help you clean it and put spirit,' I offered.

I have already done it ma,' she replied.

Then, I admonished her to take some painkillers and left.

Later that night, I waited a long time for him to come to the room but he didn't show up. When I went in search of him, I found him at the front of the house with Blessing, who was seated in a green skirt, her foot in my husband's hand. Right beside them was one of my foster daughters, who was nine years old at the time.

'What are you people doing?' I asked.

'Helping Blessing massage her leg,' he said, without looking back at me. The entire scene looked so wrong, yet innocent, to me.

I didn't know what else to say, but I felt that familiar feeling of worthlessness rush over me in that instant. I walked up to our bedroom that evening with an intent to commit suicide. I finally concluded that I was useless to the world if my own husband would cheat on me with Blessing.

I picked up a bottle of Izal and was toying with it when the door to the room opened. It was him. I put the Izal under the bed, immediately.

'I don't like how I saw you with Blessing,' I told him.

He was immediately upset that I would misconstrue his intentions when he was just trying to help her. 'Do you know how much money you would have spent at a hospital if I didn't help her? Do you know the injury could get worse?'

'It is not in your place to take care of her leg. You are not a doctor. And even if you wanted to help, why did you have to be doing it outside in the dark?' I argued.

'Nifemi was there with us.'

'I sha don't like you helping Blessing with her leg.'

'So, I did a bad thing?' he asked, in anger.

'No, but next time I will be the one to be doing it for her. Anything with the girls, please let me be the one to handle it.'

He was visibly angry, but he didn't say more.

The next morning, I called Blessing to ask how her leg was healing and how she was, generally.

'My leg is fine ma. Everything is fine.'

'Whenever you have any issue, come to me instead of going to Uncle Toba. Do you understand?'

She nodded.

'I am a woman and I can understand your issues better. It is best we stick together,' I continued.

'Yes ma,' she responded.

'So, is there anything you want to tell me?'

'No ma.'

'Are you sure? Remember that I will always believe you no matter what.'

Those were words I had said to her many times, in the four years that she had been with me.

'I know ma. Thank you ma.'

After speaking with Blessing, I felt more at ease. If there was anything, I was confident that Blessing would have told me. She was my most trusted foster child, who loved me and would never betray me.

*

One night, I woke up at about 2 a.m. He was not by my side. This was not the first time I would wake up in the middle of the night and find myself alone in bed. After the first few times, I no longer bothered looking for him. Usually, I would just continue to sleep, but on this night, I got out of bed and headed downstairs. There was no electricity, so the house was dark. I found him sitting downstairs with his phone, playing a game. He said he couldn't sleep, so he was trying to design some shirts but his laptop died. And, so, he started playing a game.

Something wasn't right. I could feel it in my gut. But on looking around, everything seemed fine. I asked that we go back upstairs, and he obliged, but my stomach began to hurt and I started to shiver — this is how my body tells me something is off.

We laid on the bed for a few minutes, then I headed out and went to the girls' room. The moment I opened the door, Blessing turned to look at me from the top bunk and then turned away. What was she doing awake at that time? I went back to the room and laid on the bed with him. He wrapped his arms around me, but I still felt the shivers.

'Something is going on in this house,' I whispered.

He went quiet for a beat before he said, 'Like what?'

'I don't know. Something just doesn't feel right.'

He held me tighter and snuggled closer. For a few seconds, we were quiet, listening to the silent darkness. Then finally, he spoke.

'I know you think I am having an affair with Blessing and I don't know if I should be insulted or angry that you would think so low of me.'

He was right. I thought there was an affair. However, his words made me feel ridiculous for entertaining such thoughts, so I apologised.

'I didn't mean to insult or upset you, please. I am only trying to protect you. I think you should reduce the way you play with her, so that she won't have any excuse to accuse you of rape or sexual abuse in the future.'

'You are right,' he agreed.

In truth, I wasn't trying to protect him. I was more concerned about Blessing.

The next morning, I called her for a chat. I repeated our sex education conversation and made her promise to tell me if she was having any issues. She agreed, and assured me that she was fine.

*

We were to attend a dance class with my kids, at Lekki, one Saturday morning. When I stepped out of the house, I met him scrutinizing the bonnet of his car. I moved closer, wondering what had happened.

'Rat has entered the bonnet of the car,' he said, worry lines forming on his face.

'How do you know?' I asked.

He showed me grains of raw rice around the engine. 'See. It is only rats that can bring it here.'

I wondered why a rat would eat raw rice and how the rat carried the raw rice from wherever to the bonnet.

'Rats these days are not smiling,' he said.

I laughed in agreement.

Through the next few weeks, he continued to complain about the rats bringing food to his car bonnet.

On a Sunday morning, right before we went to church, he brought me and my kids to his car bonnet to show us a raw snail, and grains of rice in his car engine.

'See what the rats did again,' He said.

We were amused. At this point, I really did believe the rats were moving mad.

'Is the rat trying to make stew?' one of my girls commented, to which we all laughed, but he still looked worried.

'They might start eating my car engine. With this one now, the car might not even start,' he said.

He went behind the wheel and tried to start the car. It did not start. He got out of the car.

'What will we do now?' I asked.

'I think they come out at midnight so I will be coming to warm up the car every midnight so that it is too hot for them.'

I agreed with him.

A few minutes later, the car engine started.

*

I had given my kids a phone, so that I could contact them if need be, and so they could also contact me. I started to notice that Blessing always had the phone with her. I also noticed that the credit I purchased on the phone would mysteriously disappear and each time I confronted Blessing about this, she always seemed confused. She couldn't seem to understand why the phone credit would run out so quickly. She also didn't make any attempt to stop holding on to the phone all the time. I assumed this was an age thing — she had turned 19 and I figured she liked the feel of 'having' a phone.

So, I let it be; until Toba started to complain.

It took me a while to notice his obsessive worry and need to monitor Blessing, which I found, rather, silly. It became obvious when he would suddenly offer to pick my kids from school to 'surprise' them. Then, he would say he wanted to check on Blessing on her way back from school because he suspected that she had a boyfriend, which was why she had started coming back late from school.

'She is old enough to have a boyfriend if she wants to, as long she can focus on her studies and stop failing,' I told him.

He didn't agree with me. He wanted to know what she was doing, always. Then, he complained that she was always with the phone, suggesting that the credit on the phone was finishing so quickly, because she was calling someone with it.

So, he continued to monitor her, while I monitored him.

*

One day, we were alone in the house; I was upstairs, and he was downstairs. The lights went off and came back on, and I assumed it was PHCN. Later that night, I tried to turn on the TV his brother had gifted us but it didn't come on. I called his attention to this.

When he came around to look at it, we found that everything connected to the TV socket had spoilt — the TV, DSTV and CCTV. Despite the many other gadgets in the house, I found it strange that only those ones developed a fault. He agreed with me that it was a rather strange occurrence, but blamed it on PHCN.

I decided we'd fix the CCTV DVR, so we got a technician.

'The DVR can never get bad from a small current surge. Except someone tampered with the DVR,' the technician said.

Later that night, before we slept, he repeated what the technician said.

'Who would mess with the DVR?' I wondered aloud. 'Nobody enters this room except us.'

'Are we buying another one?' he asked.

'No. I cannot afford that right now,' I replied.

Much later, that night of July 8th, when everything began to fall apart, he would use the spoilt CCTV DVR as an excuse. He would say over and over, 'I wish the CCTV was working so you'd see I wasn't talking to Blessing' even though they had been talking.

Now, I am convinced he tampered with the CCTV and DVR because he had everything planned out and he didn't need CCTV footage being used against him.

*

Another day, we went to a supermarket to buy some items. When we left the house, I had my phones and MiFi with me, but when we got back to the house, I realised my MiFi was missing. I was worried that I left it at the supermarket so we went back to check; it was not there. My husband insinuated that one of the attendants may have taken it.

After unsuccessful attempts at finding it, I bought a new one.

A couple of weeks later, he found my MiFi by the side of the driver's seat. I was shocked when he told me where he found it. I wondered how it got there and why it took buying a new one to find it. He seemed as curious as I was.

But I was glad to have the MiFi back.

A few days later, he asked if he could have the new MiFi since I had found the old one. I said yes.

*

We were planning to move back to Ikorodu. His father had a property there, where we could live with the kids. My plan was to set up a new studio in Ikorodu so that I could teach more children how to dance. I was saving up money, some of which I kept with him.

One afternoon, he left the house to run an errand for his sister. She had asked him to pick up her kids from school. This wasn't the first time he'd go on this type of errand.

After he left, I went to the corridor outside our bedroom. I was writing an episode of *Tinsel,* which I had to submit by evening. He came back a few hours later and Blessing opened the gate for him. The thing about the corridor where I sat is, you won't know anyone is seated up there except you are looking to find someone.

I watched as he drove into the compound and parked a little out of my view. I saw that he opened his car door to step out and that he had a little note in his hand, which he was reading. He put the note in his car, then took it out again. I suspected nothing, so I continued with my script.

When he came into the room, he handed me Michelle Obama's *Becoming,* which I had forgotten in his car.

'Thank you,' I said. I waited for a few seconds and then asked, 'Where is the rest?"

'Rest of what?' he asked, looking confused.

I thought he was messing with me, so I chuckled and said to him in a serious tone, 'There is something else babe.'

He laughed too. 'I just brought your book that you left in the car.'

He never lied to me — at least that is what he had made me believe — so at this point I was confused. I knew I saw him read a note. His lying strengthened my resolve to know more about the note and why he was lying about it.

'I saw you read a note downstairs and I want to see it,' I said to him.

He gave me a small smile. 'It's just a letter I wrote to tell you how much I love you. But I have already told you that now, so no need to give you the note.'

I insisted on seeing the letter. 'I want to read it myself.'

'Fine. I was only trying to protect you. The truth is, the thing in the letter will hurt you.'

'I still want to see it.'

He grew annoyed at my insistence. 'I will NOT show you the letter,' he said stubbornly.

'I want to see it.'

He ignored me. He took off the brown shorts he was wearing and hung them on the wall. Then he told me, point blank, that he would not show me the letter, before laying on the bed.

I could see the determination on his face, and at this point, I sensed that there was more to the letter than he was letting on. I just wanted to know what was so important and why he felt the need to hide it from me.

So, I pestered him. He got off the bed, put on his shorts and made to head out. I ran to the door to block his path. 'Until I see the note, you are not going anywhere.'

I locked the door and put the key in my pocket.

He chuckled mirthlessly, then went to the balcony and climbed the railing. 'If you don't stop disturbing me, I am going to jump down.'

He looked like he was going to do it; I panicked and let him be. I went back to the bedroom door to return the key.

I followed him outside the room, insisting on seeing the letter and its content. We walked down the estate and back to the house. All the while, I walked behind him, demanding to know what was in the letter. By the time we got back to the house, I was exhausted and at the verge of giving up, but seeing how far he was willing to go for this letter made me determined to see it.

Once we were back in the room, I made to check his shorts. He pushed me away forcefully and in one swift movement, he took the letter out of his pocket and threw it in his mouth. As I watched him chew the note, I could feel my own anger seething. I pushed him back, frustrated, but he didn't budge. He continued to chew on the letter, looking me straight in the eye. It was final. I was never going to know what was in that letter. When he was done chewing, he spat into the dustbin and stepped out.

My heart sank. I was weak. I knew Blessing gave him that letter. And I knew for sure that he was lying to me and hiding things from me. I felt betrayed that the person I loved and trusted would do that to me.

What is the purpose of life, I asked myself again. I went downstairs to the first aid box, my eyes heavy with tears, and took out some drugs. I went back to our room and sent him a message, thanking him for all he had done. Then, I started to swallow the pills one after the other, wailing as I popped them.

After I had swallowed the 7th tablet, he walked into the room, and pulled me away from the drugs.

'Let me go!' I yelled.

He held on to me, took me downstairs and offered me a cup of palm oil.

'I am going to call your sister,' he said.

'Don't call her,' I said, as I sat, glaring at him. 'Remember you chewed up that letter.'

That devilish half-smile appeared on his face. 'The letter was some of the kids writing that they don't want to live with you anymore. Blessing gave it to me.'

It made no sense. If that was the content, why didn't he just give it to me? Why would Blessing tell him instead of me? He didn't provide answers to my questions. Instead, he took out his phone and showed me something on a betting site.

He had gone betting with the money I saved up with him and lost all of it. My money was gone. Two million naira!

I flung the glass of palm oil on the floor.

That was my lightbulb moment. I knew in that instant that this man would be the death of me. I was also certain that he could not be an equal partner on my project.

CHAPTER SEVEN

HOW I GOT AWAY FROM MY MURDER

"So often victims end up unnecessarily prolonging their abuse because they buy into the notion that their abuser must be coming from a wounded place and that only patient love and tolerance (and lots of misguided therapy) will help them heal."
— George K. Simon

That night of July 8, 2019, after my husband tried to kill me, I was still undecided. One half of me had no plans of leaving him, because I was afraid I would never find anyone to love and tolerate me the way he did. The other half wanted to leave because I knew he would destroy me.

By the next day, which was a Tuesday, I was on the verge of losing my mind at the thought of Blessing and my husband having an affair, the sheer betrayal and the fact that Blessing didn't trust me enough to tell me what was going on. I thought about how long it must have been going on for, and the way they came up with lie after lie until they could no longer deny it. I kept on asking myself if I was so inadequate and terrible that he would choose a barely literate 19-year-old over me. I wanted to talk to someone, I needed to.

When I discussed this with him, he said, 'You know we agreed that we will not have a third party in our marriage.'

I nodded in agreement. We had both agreed to this, which was why I never told anyone about all the money he would borrow and never return, and the unnecessary expenses he would convince me to give in to.

I was dying inside and I didn't even have a chance to call someone in secret, because he would not let me out of his sight.

*

Our trip to Egypt was the next day. Since we were unable to get the yellow cards before the trip, I made some enquiries and found that our next best option was to get them at the airport. I decided we would pick them up the next morning; I was sure that if we got there in good time, we would not miss our scheduled flight. But before then, I needed to print the travel tickets. Toba insisted on following me to the printer's shop. As we walked down the street of the estate, fear was my true companion.

The events of the previous day would continue to replay in my mind. I remembered being locked up. I remembered how he had put a pillow over my face three times with my hands pinned underneath my buttocks. I remembered the way he smiled when I begged him not to kill me. I could not shake the vivid, spine-chilling memory of him bringing the Sniper into the room and asking me to drink it. I knew it was only a matter of time before I died at his hands.

I looked up to him with sad and fearful eyes. 'You will kill me.'

'Never,' he said. Then, he apologised for the previous day. 'I let my anger get the best of me. It will never happen again.'

'You will end up killing me as long as we are together. Even if it's five years from now,' I said.

'Please don't say that. I would never do that,' he said. I shivered as we continued to walk down the road.

Then, I heard someone yell from a moving vehicle, 'Big Head!' Only one person called me that.

I followed the voice and saw my sister waving at me from a black car, which belonged to one of her friends. I waved back, giddy with excitement. I was grateful to be alive to see my sister again. I wanted to run after the car to give her a hug. I wanted to tell her all that had happened and beg her to take me and my kids away from my monstrous husband.

But I didn't do that.

The trip was the next day; Seun and Nifemi would get the opportunity to fly in an airplane. It was one of the biggest breakthroughs for Dream Catchers — our first international trip. I needed to get myself together, and make sure we made the trip.

When we got back home with the printed tickets, I still felt like I was going to run mad. I begged him to let me speak with someone, anyone; I explained why I needed to. He gave in but insisted that I could only speak with my mum.

*

My mum was in the United States at the time. I called her to recount my experience with Blessing and my husband the previous day. I wanted to tell her how he tried to kill me too, but I decided on a piecemeal approach.

When I finished speaking, she responded in Yoruba, 'I understand what is happening but just let it go. You hear me?'

My heart sank. 'Disappointed' isn't a strong enough word to describe how I felt. I had expected her to condemn him for having an affair with such a young girl — a girl I was mentoring.

She asked me to give the phone to him, so I did. I only heard his side of the conversation, which was also in Yoruba. He smiled as he spoke.

'Good afternoon ma... nothing like that... I look at Blessing like a 12-year-old... she even calls me daddy... I lied that I didn't see Blessing because I thought they were tricking me... I thought both of them had planned something ... thank you ma... I will be more careful ma... I won't be too friendly with girls ma...'

He returned my phone to me, and my mum asked to speak with Blessing. I summoned Blessing and gave her the phone.

'Grandma wants to talk to you,' I said.

115

She took the phone and went inside her room to speak with my mum. A few minutes later, she returned my phone. My mum was still on the phone.

My stomach had begun to hurt again. I went inside to get some milk to soothe the pain as I continued to listen to her. She was still speaking in Yoruba.

'Just leave it as it is. Don't mention it anymore. The fact that you have seen a man that will stay with you — with this your children's ministry — is the Lord's doing. Most women in ministry always lose their marriage. They never have any man to call the crown of their head. Just leave the matter like that.'

'Okay ma,' I said, helpless and exhausted.

I did not tell her that he tried to kill me with Sniper, that he put his hands on my neck when we were downstairs, that he tried to suffocate me with a pillow. I realised it was pointless. She would blame me for pushing him to do those things or blame me for letting the Devil enter my home.

I thanked her for the advice and, strangely enough, I felt better afterwards. I decided to heed mummy's words of admonition — to stay in my marriage because no other man might want me.

*

Although I had resolved to stay with my husband, I was still terrified that he tried to kill me and I was worried he'd do it again. I needed to tell someone about the attempted murder. Someone, who could save me if things got out of hand. Someone, who could help me.

I thought long and hard and Niran came to mind; he was the only one I could think of. Since he had called me the day before and couldn't get through because Toba was torturing me at the time, I reasoned I could use the opportunity to explain that I didn't forget my phone at home like I said when I called him back — that I was actually locked up. He was a big, muscular man. I believed he could come to my rescue.

I knew I had to be careful; my husband could seize my phone at any time.

So, I created a new email account on my iPhone. I asked Niran for his email address on WhatsApp and once he replied, I deleted the message.

It was the first time I realised you could schedule a message on Gmail. I sent a timed message to Niran, so that if I got locked up again, and my phone got seized, my husband would not see my cry for help, which could cause him to finally kill me.

I didn't hear back from Niran. I checked my mail ever so often, hoping to read some kind of '007' escape plan, but nothing came.

Then, I reminded myself that Niran and I were just business associates and I couldn't expect him to save me. So, I redirected my thoughts to the upcoming trip. The girls chattered in excitement as they packed their boxes, in anticipation of the journey. I psyched myself into feeling excited for the rare opportunity.

Later that day, while my husband took a shower, I received a call from a lady, asking if I was fine. She said Niran had told her I had some issues with my partner. She wanted to know if we were all able to travel, and whether my husband would still be coming on the trip.

I laughed, mirthlessly, and said, 'Yes. He is still coming and everything is fine.'. Then, I ended the call. What did she expect? That I would ask someone who almost killed me to drop out from a planned joint trip so he could suspect that I wanted to leave him, and finish off the job, once and for all?

I was upset, worried, afraid and a wreck, but I did my best to act as unsuspicious as possible.

*

The trip to Egypt remains the worst trip of my life, the only highlight being that two of my girls got to live one of their biggest dreams, which was to travel outside Nigeria on an airplane. Otherwise, I was lost in thoughts and scared, for the most part.

Niran had travelled with us, and I secretly hoped he would rescue me at some point — throw a punch at my husband, confront him for being a terrible man — anything but nothing.

I don't know why I thought this innocent young man minding his business would be my saviour, but I was desperate for one. When we got our room placements, Niran put me on a different floor from my husband, but my husband demanded for a switch so that we could remain on the same floor.

Once we were settled with the rooms, I informed my husband that I had to stay in the room with the girls as they couldn't stay in a room alone. To my surprise, he agreed. But he stayed with us in the room for a long while before leaving. The moment he left, I quickly searched for my birth control pills, which I had sneaked into my waist purse and threw one in my mouth.

Throughout the trip, I did my best to avoid Toba but he was constantly overbearing. When he asked that we take pictures together, I said no. Then, he frowned, and I got scared, so I agreed to the pictures. When he handed me a drink of water, I refused to take it. He insisted and I got scared, so I took it from him.

The night before we left Egypt, he came to the room I shared with the girls to ask if I could come to his room — he was horny and it would only take a short time, after which I could return to the girls, he said. I lied that I had a stomach upset and that I also had to keep an eye on the girls.

He stormed out of the room.

Sometimes, I wonder if he would have strangled me to death mid-coitus if I had followed him that night.

*

By the end of our trip, I realised that Niran wasn't going to save me. On the plane back, my husband sent me messages about how he missed me — I knew this meant sex; I knew I had to get away, but I didn't know how.

When we landed in Nigeria and navigated the airport to finalise departure protocols, I racked my brain for who else I could speak to.

I thought of Nkiru, a passionate individual, feminist and my boss, who helped me get through my lowest moments and had become a big sister to me. I decided I would reach out to her.

In the Uber, I opted to sit at the back with the girls. While he sat in front, I took out my phone and sent a timed email to Nkiru from my new account — I, basically, copied the email I had sent to Niran and forwarded same to Nkiru.

Hi,

Something happened in my house on Monday morning. I was supposed to run off at some point but I couldn't because of the AFCON Egypt trip. I have worked so hard for so many years that this breakthrough I have to see it through.

As I was saying, something happened so I told my partner I was done dealing with his BS and I wanted to end things. He begged and apologized and said I was misunderstanding things. I ignored and began speaking to a lawyer friend to know what it takes to annul a 9 months marriage.

While I was chatting my partner snatched my phone and saw my messages to the lawyer. I tried to collect the phone but he wouldn't give it back. This resulted in a 30 minutes scuffle between both of us cos I really wanted my phone back. He wouldn't give it back. I might have over done it by holding his cloths because of course my strength cannot match his. Long story short; he seized my two phones for hours.
While I was trying to get him to give my phone, he locked both of us up in the room

and said we'd stay together. I screamed but I
wasn't let out. Eventually I was let out still
without my phone. I went to another room,
minutes later he came over and asked that he
wants to show me something. I followed into
the room and then he locked us up again.
Saying till death do us part. He also brought
sniper into the room. He put a pillow over my
face twice although he did not press it down.
He suggested it. Later he calmed down and
said he could never kill me or hurt me.
Eventually, He gave me my phone at some
point.

He asked why I wanted to leave him. I said I
didn't want to leave anymore that we should
start afresh because I was just so scared. I
took one of the boys to the clinic and began
chatting with my lawyer friend.
I didn't know he had hacked my phone and he
could read messages I was texting on whats
app.
Back home I went into the room to take some
water, he came in and locked me in again.
Saying I lied to him that I'm still planning on
leaving him.
He lied that he had taken some pills and he
would die soon and made me lie beside him
while he acted like he was dying. I was scared

cos I thought he was really going to die. I
cried and screamed. Tried to gather myself
then lost it again. He put a pillow over my face
for the third time. He pressed it for 2 seconds
this time and I begged and reminded him it
was me. He took off the pillow.
I told him I was hungry and hadn't eaten all
day he said that's my problem that he couldn't
let me out.
 I gave up eventually and he later allowed me
to eat at about 10:30pm. He followed me and
made sure I followed him back to the room. I
gave up. I just wanted us to make it till
Wednesday.
Next morning I got some freedom back and
he apologized. I think I am having Stockholm
Syndrome. He says he will never do it again. I
know I hear about these stories and read
online and I judge the women. Here I am.
All my life I have had bad luck with men. Even
though I barely dated anyone out of fear.

I don't know why I am telling you this. I did
not know who to tell. I can't tell my family yet.
I don't know what to do. I was going to run off
once we got back from Egypt. How do I run
with 10kids?
I'm scared.
I feel pity for him. I feel fear for him.

I'm scared.
I feel pity for him. I feel fear for him.
I don't know what to do.
I don't want him to know I'm talking to anyone
cos I promised not to tell anyone. But I know I
don't know how to take care of myself or think
about what's best for me.

I'll take any advice but please be calm. I can't
take calls. Just conversation on here.

Shit! Feels like a movie or dream.
I didn't see any signs. I didn't before now.

She responded in minutes:

When we got back home, he pulled me into our room and started to apologise again.

'I have missed you so much,' he said, pulling me into a hug. I stiffened. I could feel his erection on my thigh.

'I want us to start all over again. I promise to be a good husband.'

I nodded. If I got a dollar for every time he said that to me, I'd have bought a small plot of land in Ikorodu.

He started to kiss me. I barely stood there, unresponsive. I don't think he cared. He pulled me towards the bed and I lay on my back. He poured some oil on his penis and then, slid into me.

I chanted to myself, repeatedly, *'You really are just a hole to be fucked. So just stay till he is done.'*

'Do you like it?' he asked, as he rocked me.

A tear dropped from my eyes, and then there were two and three and a river of tears. I wiped them as they came; I didn't know what he'd do if he realised I didn't like it.

He grunted as he came; then, fell to the side of the bed and held me.

I lay there quietly, wondering if Nkiru had sent me another mail.

*

Once I got the chance, I checked my phone and saw an email from Nkiru. I handled my phone discreetly, so he would not catch me while I was typing a reply to her emails.

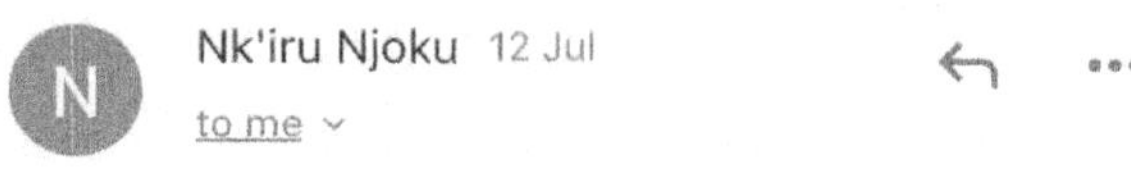

First thing you must do is tell your parents and siblings. How does that sit with you?

And where were the kids when all this was happening?
--

--

Nk'iru. Njoku

I'm worried about the drama that will come from telling them.
My mum will say it is the manifestation of the devil and ask that we start praying and fasting. She will most likely have the backing of my dad and sister.
My other 3 brothers will flip. And I'm scared of what will happen when he finds out I told them and that I've been fooling him all along.

Some of the kids were in school. One of the older girls was at home. They got back from school but I was in the room and i don't know what they know. I asked a few and they seem to think I was ill on that day.

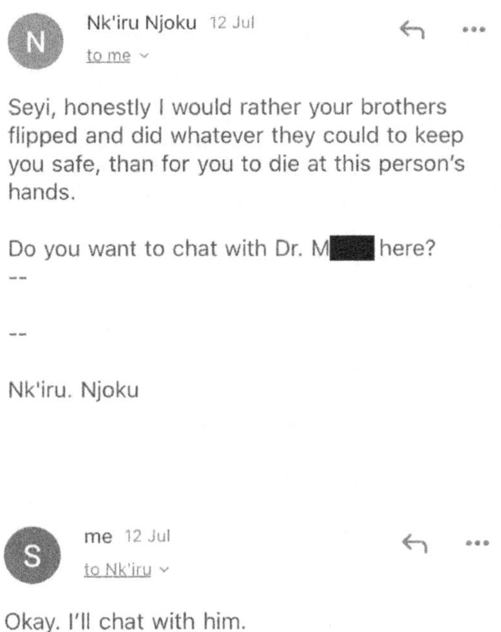

Dr. Murphy was a therapist, who was also like a big uncle to me. I knew he would treat my conversations with him in confidentiality. I narrated my ordeal to him via timed emails, and he tried to convince me to leave. I didn't see that happening.

I was featured on INSTYLE magazine's 50 Badass Women and the day we returned from the Egypt trip was the same day the publication came out. That night, I read and showed the article to my kids; they were proud of me. Although, I was broken inside, I tried to find joy in my little wins.

I showed it to him too. He smiled that creepy half-smile; I knew he wasn't happy for me.

I didn't get a chance to use my phone discreetly that night.

The next morning was a Saturday. An email from Nkiru was waiting in my inbox.

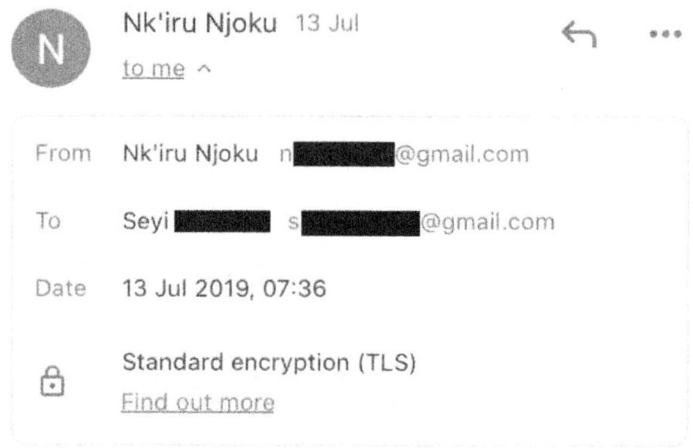

Hi Seyi.

K███ has told me how far you guys have discussed.

Listen, Stockholm syndrome is a thing and I'm happy you're aware of it and have self-diagnosed yourself with it. But that's a minor issue we can discuss later.

Right now, you have to save yourself and get out of that space. Forget about whether he will try to look for you or not. We are happy to make it a security issue and invite the police or a women's rights group if need be. And there are many of them.

Forget about waiting until the children go on holiday. They are not in university. Missing one week of school won't kill them.

There's a house in ikorodu waiting for you and the kids RIGHT NOW.

It's ljeoma's father's house. I had to give her a very tiny hint and I hope you won't mind because I'm focused on having you safe and sound, as well as the kids.

Please please I beg you in the name of anything you hold dear. Think of YOURSELF, and not of him. We've seen many stories like this and YOU WILL NOT BE A STATISTIC.

Seyi do you hear me?! You will not be a statistic.

I'm ready to speak to ljeoma and another friend, to come and get you guys out of there IMMEDIATELY.

Please forget how your hubby will feel. We will take it the whole nine yards as far as your protection is concerned.

This thing has happened to so many people

Seyi do you hear me?! You will not be a
statistic.

I'm ready to speak to Ijeoma and another
friend, to come and get you guys out of there
IMMEDIATELY.

Please forget how your hubby will feel. We will
take it the whole nine yards as far as your
protection is concerned.

This thing has happened to so many people
and this is exactly how it started. He has no
value for his own life, and feels like he has
nothing to lose. Therefore your own life is
ABSOLUTELY nothing to him, no matter what
he tells you.

Seyi GET OUT NOW.
--

--

Nk'iru. Njoku

If I'm being sincere, I felt she was blowing the ordeal
out of proportion. I found her reaction quite amusing,
that I chuckled while reading some of her emails. I
thought of every excuse in the book as I wondered why I
told her of my predicament in the first place. I couldn't
see what she was seeing. All I saw and understood was
that my husband had made a mistake and he had
apologised.

I responded to her email.

Eh.
Good morning.
Can we leave tomorrow after the show ? I can discreetly pack some things in a bag when we are leaving so that we can go from there maybe.
We are presently in Lekki for a dance class.
I would rather leave discreetly but I understand having to go the nine yards if necessary.
If it's something with too much attention and me packing and saying and leaving; he will try to manipulate me and I will most likely fall for that moment again.
If he carries sniper and starts drinking in front of me; I'll lose my mind. Because I'll forever feel responsible.

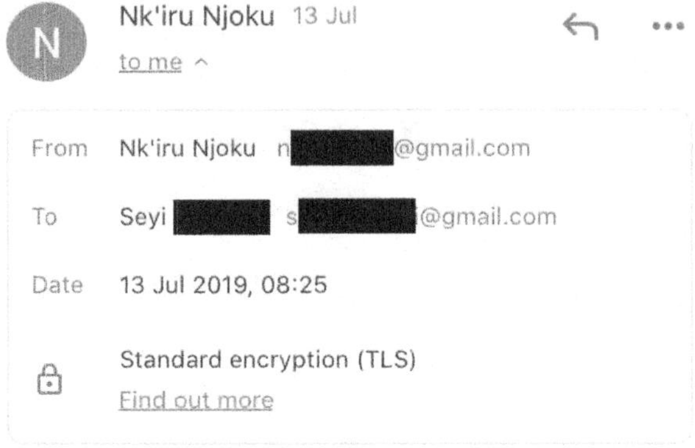

Yes you can leave tomorrow after the show. I'll put ijeoma on notice. Where is the show? Would you need to be picked up?
--

--

Nk'iru. Njoku

All the while, I glanced around the house furtively, monitoring his movement and making sure he would not catch me unawares and seize my phone again.

As I write, I feel a greater sense of gratitude and love towards Nkiru. I don't know how she coped with my excuses. If I were in her shoes, I would have left me alone; I am glad she isn't me. She would later tell me she did not do it alone, and for that, I feel just as grateful to Dr. M, Nkiru's partner; Ijeoma Ogwuegbu, S.K,, and Nneka, colleagues and friends to Nkiru, all of whom Nkiru sought counsel from, every step of the way, to come up with my getaway plan.

I got a mail from Dr M███. Another better was is he makes T-shirts. So maybe if someone called and gave him a deal to make some shirts, he would go to the market to buy materials then I can use that time to quickly pack some things. Because with the gig, he will come with us. And he will wonder why the unnecessary packing of items.
The only thing that gets him out of the house is work. To make shirts.
That gets him out. Or when his family call to ask for his help. But family angle may not work now.
So probably the shirt thing. Can we get someone call to order actual shirts from him. Like 5. It needs to be a substantial number for him to be able to moveable get it done.
He will do the shirt for like 4K. If they agree to that price he will agree to do it. But there has to be a bargain too.

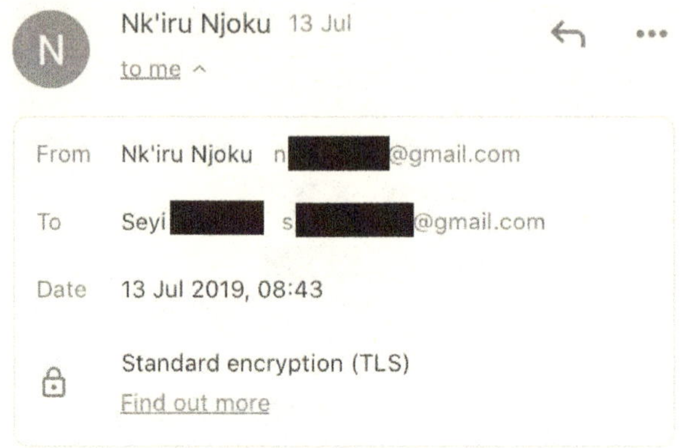

Will he go to get shirts on a Sunday?
--

--

Nk'iru. Njoku

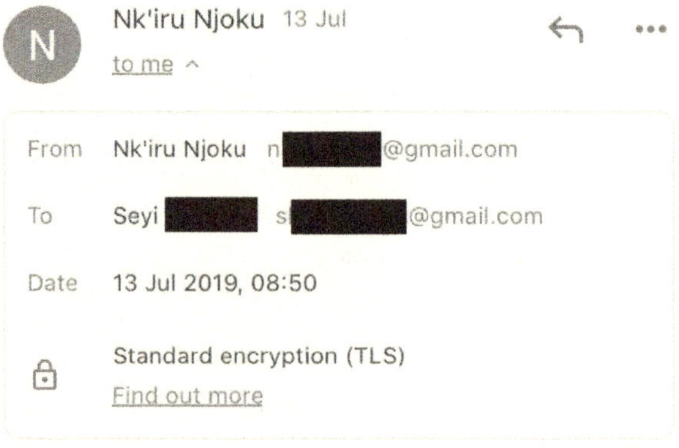

Or should we make the call for shirts today?

Our best bet would be on Monday. He also designs website and a meeting can keep him out for a few hours. A meeting on the island or something.
But I don't know how one can say they got his contact. He designed the dream catchers website but it's just his name on there.
If he gets a call today on either shirt or website, for shirt - deadline will be like Wednesday so that he can quickly go to the market on Monday or Tuesday and deliver on Wednesday.
For the website a call today to fix a meeting for Monday. Whichever of the two.

I can keep him sweet for a few more days. As long as I'm acting normal and try not to start an argument or any sorts. Also what he is a expecting is a lawyer and divorce hearing.

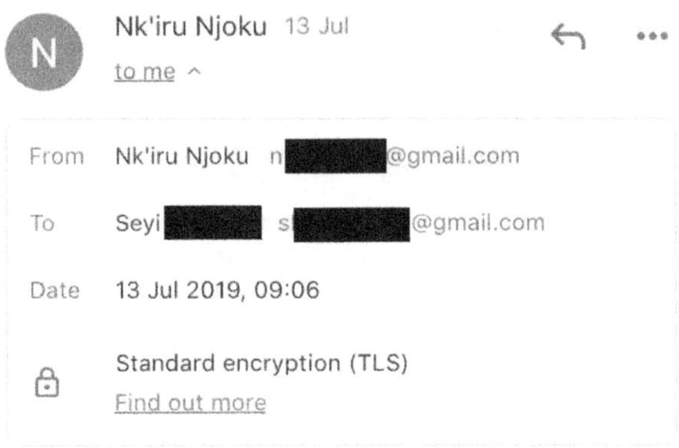

Nk'iru Njoku 13 Jul

to me ^

From	Nk'iru Njoku n███████@gmail.com
To	Seyi █████ s█████████@gmail.com
Date	13 Jul 2019, 09:06

Standard encryption (TLS)
Find out more

Here's what we are thinking: what about if you leave from the show tomorrow and then your family can go get your things afterwards?

You can pick up your laptop which is very essential. We don't want him to destroy it.

I can send you script breakdowns and give you instructions to write them today/tomorrow. So you can take it with you and be typing in the car or something.

I'll also put a message on your WhatsApp scolding you and your team for story d and asking you to make urgent changes which must be submitted on Monday early morning.

So that this can justify why you need your
laptop. Anything else can be picked up later
as we decide. We don't want you staying with
him more than today.

Please.

Ijeoma and a driver will wait for you at the
performance place. Give me the address right
now, and the time of the performance.

--

--

Nk'iru. Njoku

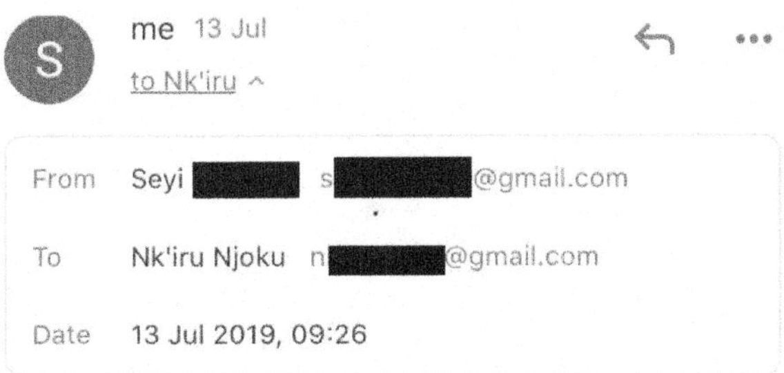

he will be at the show and it will be difficult
for the 1 1 of us to sneak away without him
noticing and causing a scene.

Nk'iru Njoku 13 Jul
to me ⌄

You won't need to sneak. The driver is 6ft 5.

Ijeoma will be there. They will put you in the vehicles and tell him to stand back.

Seyi you have to stop worrying about the external things like how people will see it or how he will feel.

Please confirm to me that you get this and are ready to go with it.

--

--

Nk'iru. Njoku

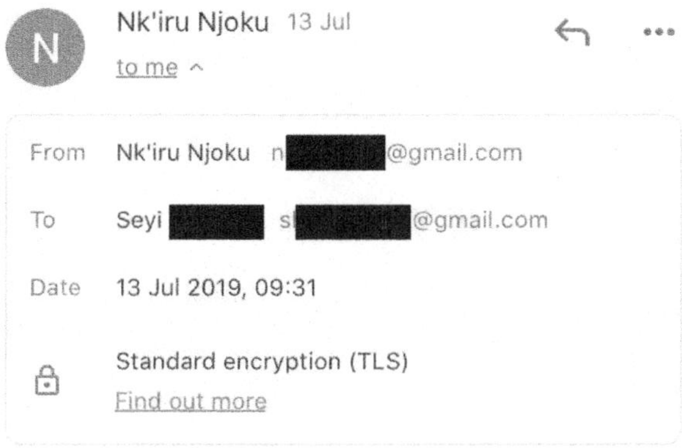

If you insist that Monday is better for you to leave, we can distract him with a meeting. But will he not take your phones away from you? Since he won't be around you. I feel he may want to take your phones.

That's why I'm seeing the post-performance separation as best.

Tell me explicitly how you feel about both scenarios.

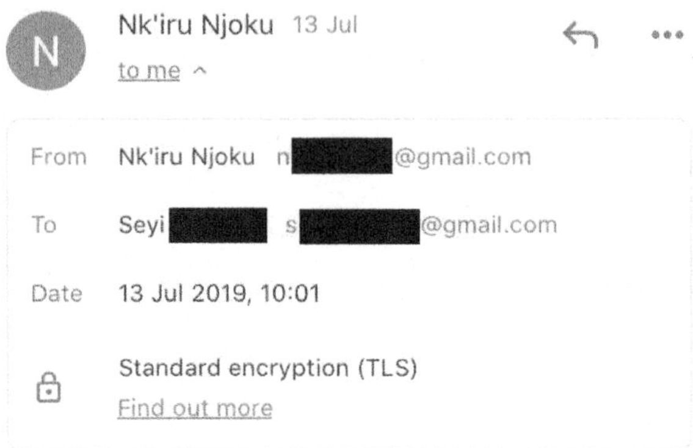

Also, where are your brothers? Seyi, you need them. Please. Let any one of them who's in town be the one to go get your things after the separation tomorrow. Think about it please.

Unfortunately for me, none of my brothers are in town. And they are the only ones I can be sure will back me up 💯!

About post performance on sunday - I feel that a lot of emotions and confusion will happen. Especially with the kids being there. And it happening all of a sudden. They will see his reaction. And it might damage them. Two of them already witnessed some scuffle on Monday. The two youngest.
He is really nice to them. So they

like him and if we just separate from him like that; it might affect them.

Monday -
I can get as many things needed
before he gets back. Including the
documents.
The kids won't know anything
asides from what i explain. My
psychology will be intact to some
extent.
I don't think he will take away my
phone. If I try to behave, he won't
take it.
The distraction just has to be good.

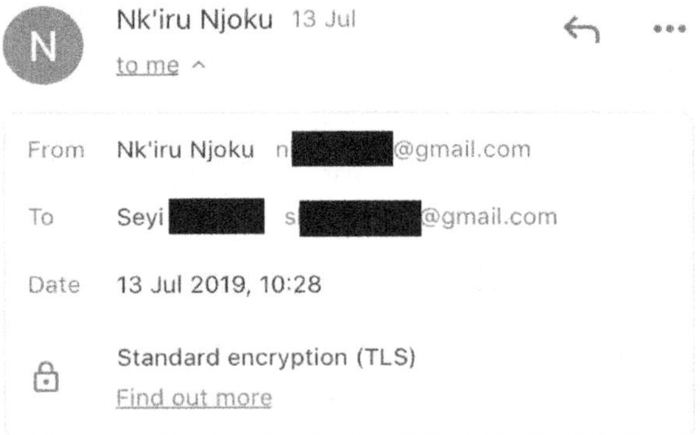

So on Monday, if we get him out of the house
then you can get the docs and leave same
day before he gets back, right?
--

--

Nk'iru. Njoku

There's an option of getting the police involved. It makes sense. A friend is ready to do this. Have him detained till Monday and you pack and leave safely.

On Sat, 13 Jul 2019 at 10:28 am, Nk'iru Njoku <n████@gmail.com> wrote:

So on Monday, if we get him out of the house then you can get the docs and leave same day before he gets back, right?
--

--

Nk'iru. Njoku

Getting him out of the house on Monday is fine. I'll leave ASAP and get the kids from school.i might just need help with transportation. We live at Magodo Isheri: No police please.

Address please.

And well organize to get him out of the house on Monday. There will be two cars to get you out and take you to the safe space.
--

--

Nk'iru. Njoku

A friend is going to call him for shirts. Does he have an insta account? Is his phone number on there? We need an explanation about where we got his number.

He has worked with B▮▮ and also D▮▮▮ (I▮▮▮▮▮) he makes a lot of shirts for I▮▮▮▮▮ so that's best bet. He shut down his Instagram.
Please ask I▮▮▮▮▮ for the number cos I▮▮▮▮▮ will know the work phone number. He has two numbers and I'm not sure which exactly he gives out to clients.

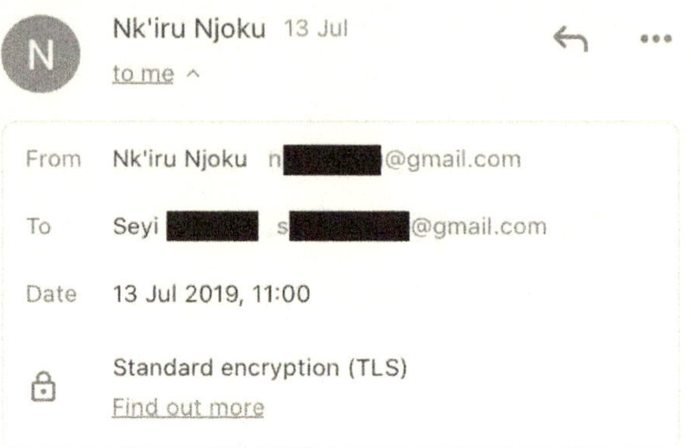

Okay. I'll ask ███████ for the number of the guy who makes shirts for him. Then we'll take it from there.

We'll call him for a meeting for Monday.
--

--

Nk'iru. Njoku

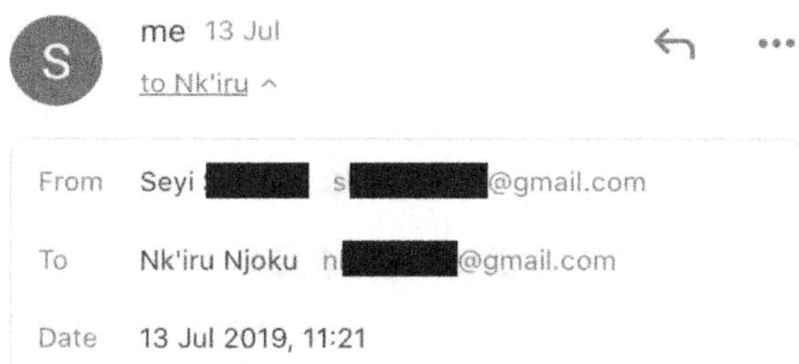

S

me 13 Jul
to Nk'iru ^

From	Seyi ██████ s███████@gmail.com
To	Nk'iru Njoku n██████@gmail.com
Date	13 Jul 2019, 11:21

Okay.
You can please send the number so I can
cross check. Cos I think I██████ has a
number of people at hand for shirts.

████████████████████

Magodo Isheri (the one by Berger)

The kids will go to school and then we will go
and pick them from school. Because if they
stay home he will suspect.

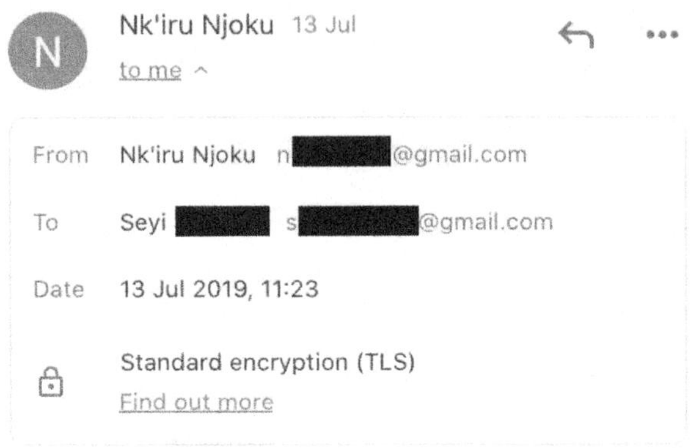

Okay cool.

We all prefer for you to get out of there today though. But I'll reach out to █ now.

\--

\--

Nk'iru. Njoku

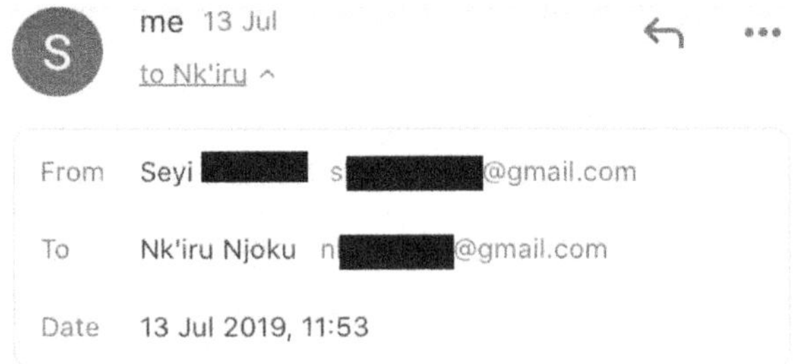

I'll stay safe promise!
Thank you sooo much. I'll speak to my brothers on Monday too.

Take a piece of paper and write out my number, ijeoma's Number, and doctor's number. Also write down emergency police number. Keep this piece of paper on your person in case he takes your phone.

--

--

Nk'iru. Njoku

I will do that.

Nk'iru Njoku 13 Jul
to me

From	Nk'iru Njoku	▮▮▮@gmail.com
To	Seyi S▮▮▮	▮▮▮@gmail.com
Date	13 Jul 2019, 13:05
🔒	Standard encryption (TLS) Find out more

▮ is not forthcoming with his number, he says he has so many and he doesn't use them much anymore. So if I have to get the number then I have to tell him what's going on which I don't want to.

Will ▮ have his number?
--

--

Nk'iru. Njoku

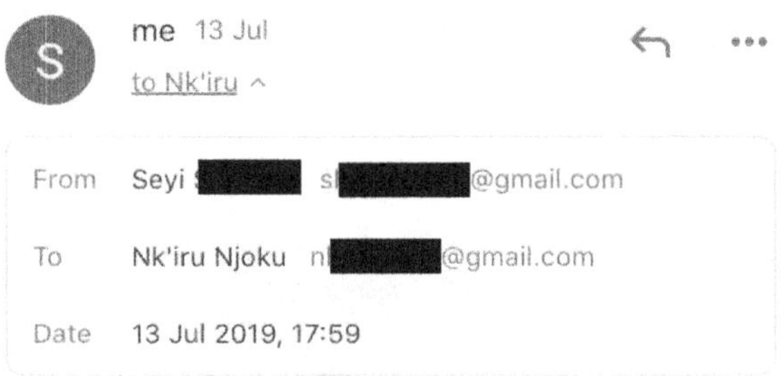

me 13 Jul
to Nk'iru

From	Seyi ▮▮▮	s▮▮▮@gmail.com
To	Nk'iru Njoku	n▮▮▮@gmail.com
Date	13 Jul 2019, 17:59

Has anyone called him?

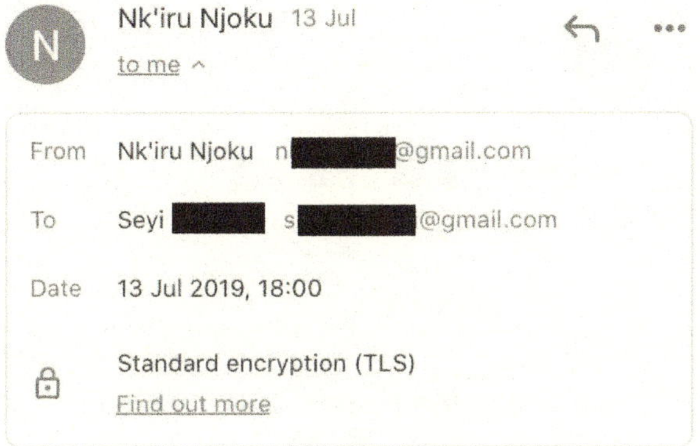

Nk'iru Njoku 13 Jul

to me ^

From	Nk'iru Njoku n███████@gmail.com
To	Seyi ████ s███████@gmail.com
Date	13 Jul 2019, 18:00
🔒	Standard encryption (TLS) Find out more

Still not able to reach B██. I███████ is not
forthcoming. Says he has lots of tee shirt
guys and doesn't want to use them again. Are
they close? If not, I can give I███████ a hint
and he can give me the number.
--

--

Nk'iru. Njoku

S

me 13 Jul

to Nk'iru ^

From	Seyi [redacted] s[redacted]@gmail.com
To	Nk'iru Njoku n[redacted]@gmail.com
Date	13 Jul 2019, 18:17

You can use the number I sent to you.
No red to talk to I[redacted].
He makes a couple of shirts so the person just needs to say 'Are you M[redacted] that makes shirts' and then make their request.
Some People know him as shirt guy.

Nk'iru Njoku 13 Jul

to me ^

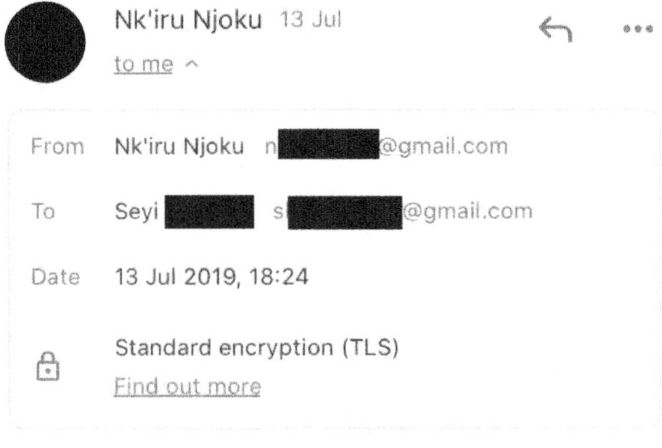

From	Nk'iru Njoku n[redacted]@gmail.com
To	Seyi [redacted] s[redacted]@gmail.com
Date	13 Jul 2019, 18:24
	Standard encryption (TLS) Find out more

Okay cool. We'll go with that.
--

--

Nk'iru. Njoku

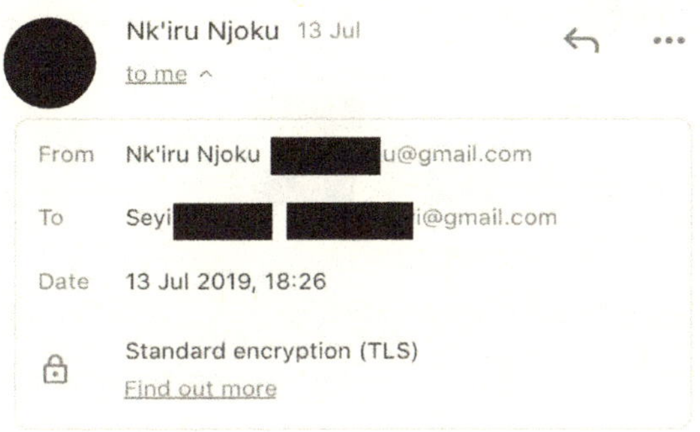

Have the children written their exams?

On Sat, 13 Jul 2019 at 6:24 pm, Nk'iru Njoku
<▓▓▓▓@gmail.com> wrote:
Okay cool. We'll go with that.
--

--

Nk'iru. Njoku

The ones who went to Egypt have a make up
to write on Monday. The others are done

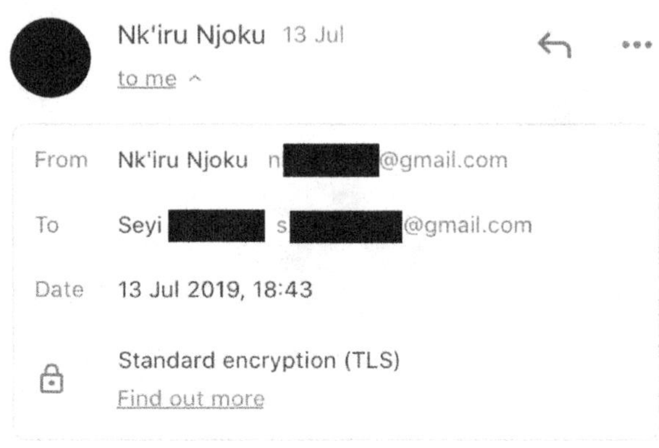

Nk'iru Njoku 13 Jul
to me

From   Nk'iru Njoku   n████████@gmail.com

To   Seyi ██████ s██████@gmail.com

Date   13 Jul 2019, 18:43

Standard encryption (TLS)
Find out more

What time is best to get him out?
--

--

Nk'iru. Njoku

me 13 Jul
to Nk'iru

Meeting time for 12 or 1 pm

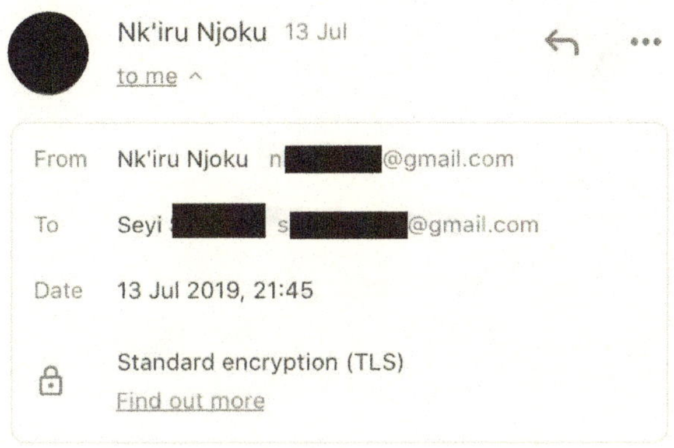

We've been calling the line but he's not picking.
--

--

Nk'iru. Njoku

Oh. He is charging it. When he gets it, I'll convince him to call back.

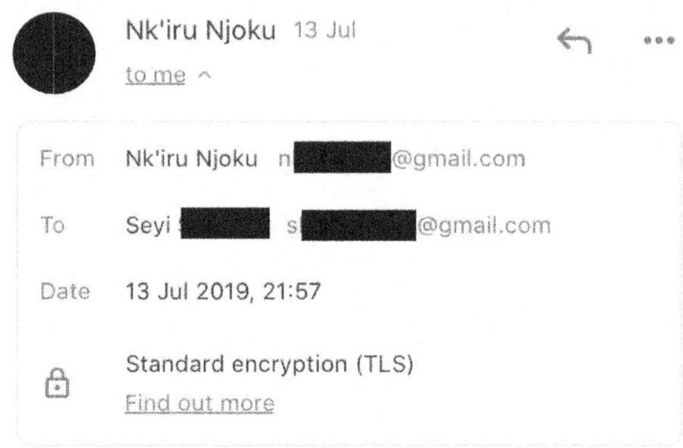

Okay. But be careful. So he doesn't wonder why you're interested.

--

--

Nk'iru. Njoku

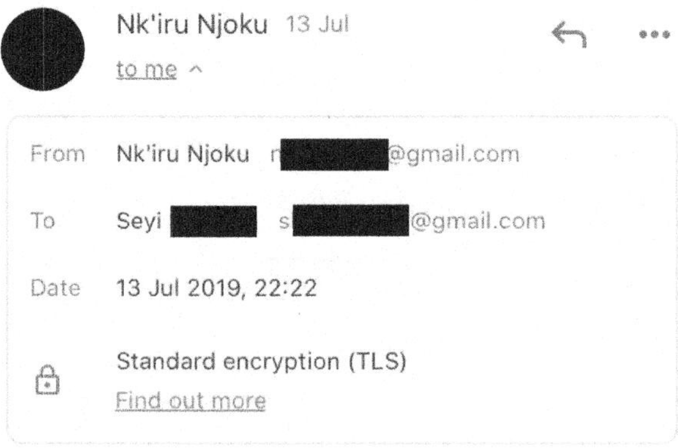

They spoke. He said he'll confirm to my friend tomorrow if he can make it.

A few minutes later, he came down to meet me to say he got a call from someone who wanted to make shirts but his instincts warned him against it.

I didn't want to convince him to go. I could not risk him getting suspicious. So, I said, 'Do what you feel is right. Just remember we need as much money as we can get.'

'Yes. But the person said he wants to make just two shirts.'

'Oh.'

'I'll decide by morning if I want to go.'

I prayed quietly that he'd choose to go by morning.

At this time, Nkiru had sent another email. I found a quiet corner to read and reply.

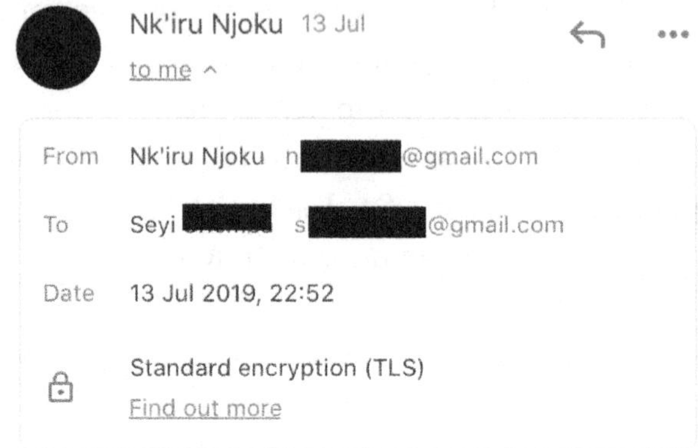

Okay. Hopefully he bites.

--

--

Nk'iru. Njoku

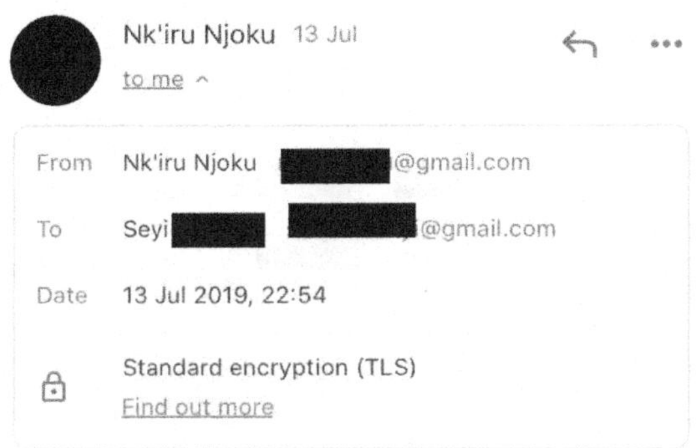

What if he decides not to go out on Monday?

On Sat, 13 Jul 2019 at 10:51 pm, Nk'iru Njoku
<r________@gmail.com> wrote:
Okay. Hopefully he bites.

--

--

Nk'iru. Njoku

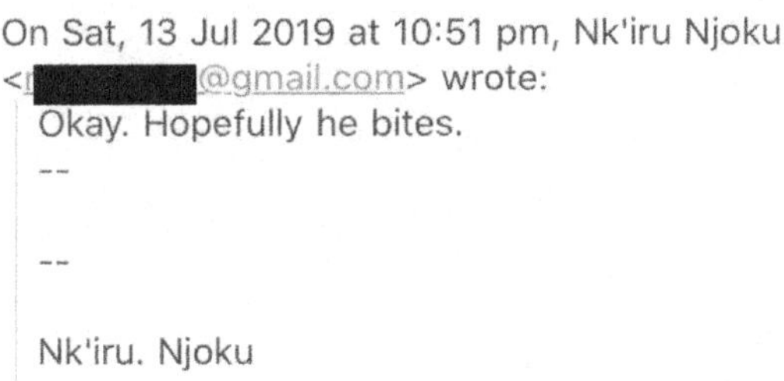

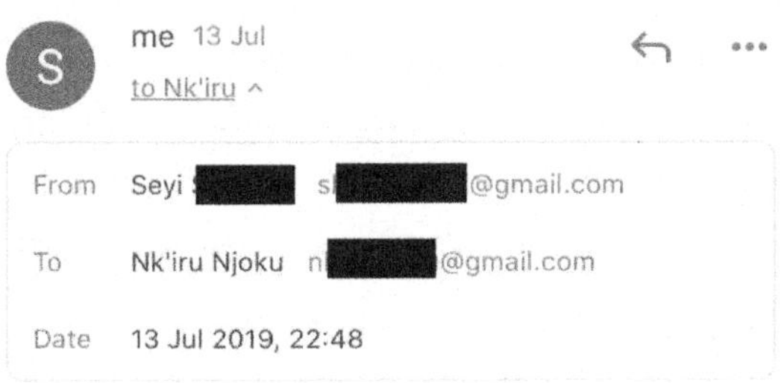

Yes he said so.
Let's see. He always researches clients.

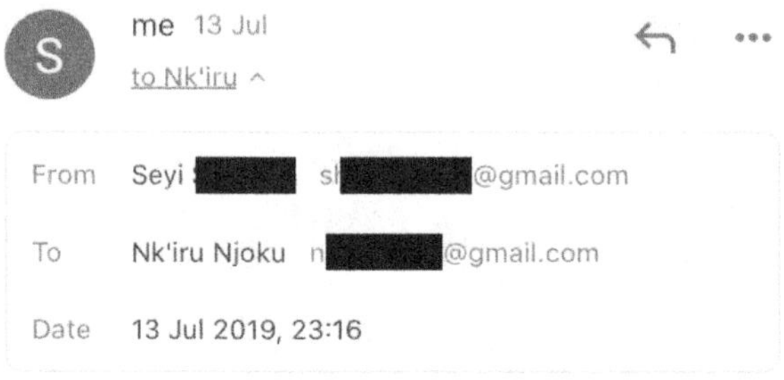

He will.
He is thinking about it already. He just wants
to be sure if it's worth his time.
But he will.

The next day was a Sunday. That morning, I summoned Blessing for a brief chat outside the house.

'Do you remember what happened on Monday?' I whispered.

'Yes ma,' she responded.

'Good. We need to leave this house, so I need you to be ready and pack a few things.'

'Shey with *Daddy Yo*?' she asked.

My heart sank. I knew for sure, then, that he had truly sunk his fangs in her and manipulated her, and she was no longer on my side. If she was, she would not have asked if we would be running off with the man that tried to kill me.

I managed a smile and said, 'Yes, but don't worry. I'll let you know later.' I knew that there was no way I could leave with her as my accomplice.

As we prepared to leave for the show, I got more emails from Nkiru.

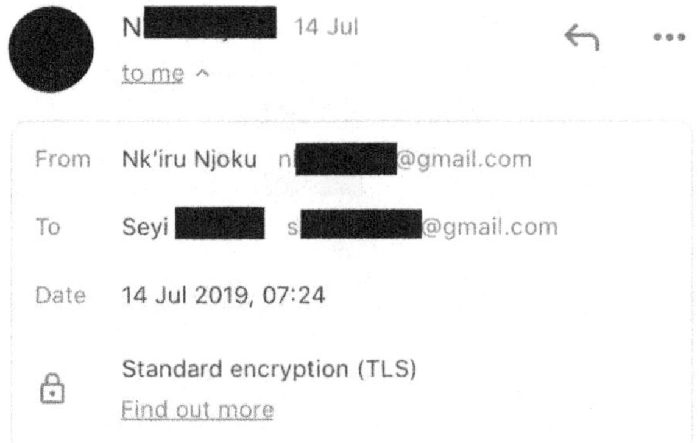

How are you?

On Sat, 13 Jul 2019 at 11:21 pm, Nk'iru Njoku <n███████@gmail.com> wrote:
> Okay
> --
>
> --
>
> Nk'iru. Njoku

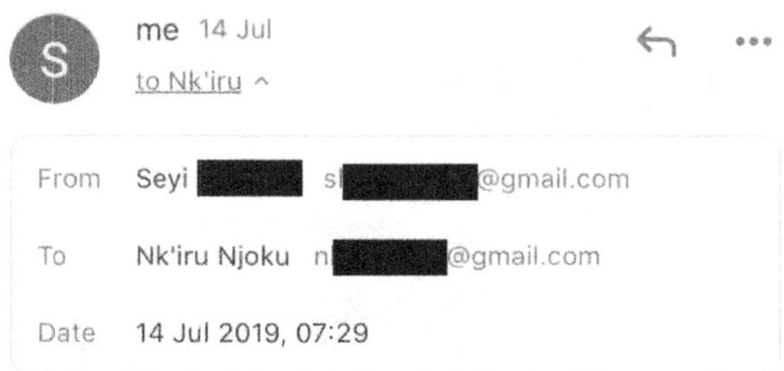

Good morning,
I am fine.! Everything is fine around here.

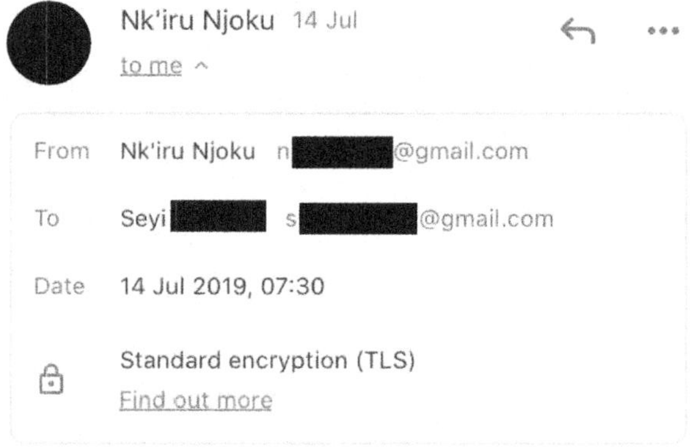

Good stuff. Take care and check in with me
now and again.
--

--

Nk'iru. Njoku

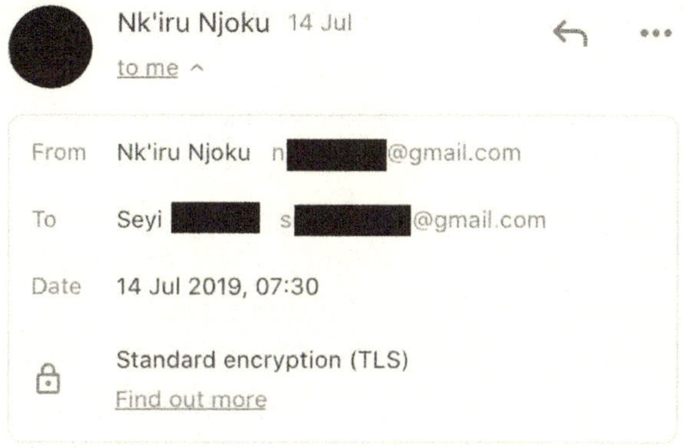

Has he made up his mind? About Monday.

I will. He hasn't made up his mind yet.
I'll keep you posted.

In the afternoon, Toba drove us to the Afroprom event, where the kids had been slated to perform. We were exiting the estate in Magodo, when he suddenly hit the accelerator. Everyone in the car screamed; we were unsure of his game plan. Then, I looked at him in fear, wondering and silently questioning if he was going to kill us all.

'Sorry, I thought you were expecting it,' he said drily.

My heart was in my mouth. I said quiet prayers, as I kept my eyes peeled for his next sudden move. I was worried he would run us into the Lagos lagoon as we drove through the Third Mainland Bridge.

When we got to the event, we were ushered into the green room. We were warmly received as different people excitedly came by to greet me and my kids. They also tried to make Toba's acquaintance but he was as cold as ice; his face, stuck in an unpleasant frown.

His strange demeanour worried me. I started to think about sending Nkiru another email to see if she could get someone to come pick us from the event. That way, we wouldn't have to return home with him. I thought about this long and hard before deciding we would leave the next morning. I just needed to figure out a way to get him out of the house by Monday afternoon.

I texted his sister to enlist her help with getting him out of the house the next day, by sending him on an errand like she used to. She asked why I wanted him out of the house. I was not sure I could tell her it was because I wanted to run away, so I told her that we were having some issues and I wanted to plan a surprise for him. She was reluctant to help but eventually said, 'Okay'.

A few minutes later, he received a call from someone I assumed to be his sister. When he dropped the call, I asked if she was the one.

'No. Why are you asking?' he replied.

I realised that I might have spoken too soon.

'Nothing. I just wanted to know,' I responded.

He looked at me suspiciously then asked, 'Why would you just ask out of nowhere if that was my sister?'

'I just wanted to know.'

'It's my dad that called.'

'Okay.'

After a beat, he asked again, 'Why did you think it was my sister? Did you tell her anything?'

'No.'

He didn't believe me.

'Give me your phone,' he demanded, anger clouding his eyes.

'No. You have no choice than to take my word for it.'

I knew he would not seize my phone in public. Even so, my heart was in my mouth. I lied that I needed to pee and left before he could respond. On my way to the bathroom, I deleted the message I had sent to his sister.

The guilt of lying overwhelmed me.

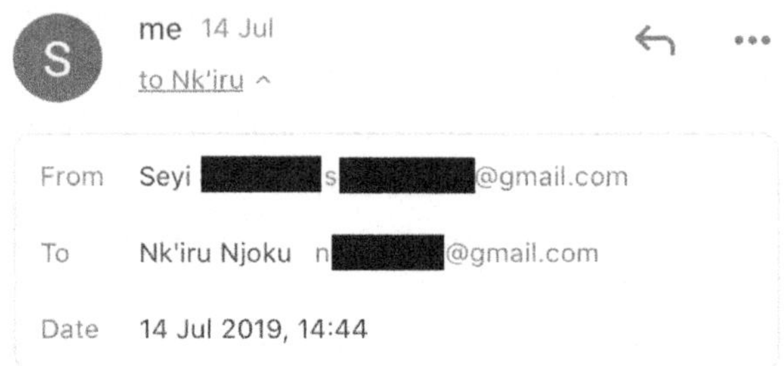

I'm not sure he will bite. So I sent a message to his sister asking if she could send him on an errand and I'll explain to her later.
She is insisting on knowing now, so I want to tell her we are planning a surprise for him.
I feel like a liar though.

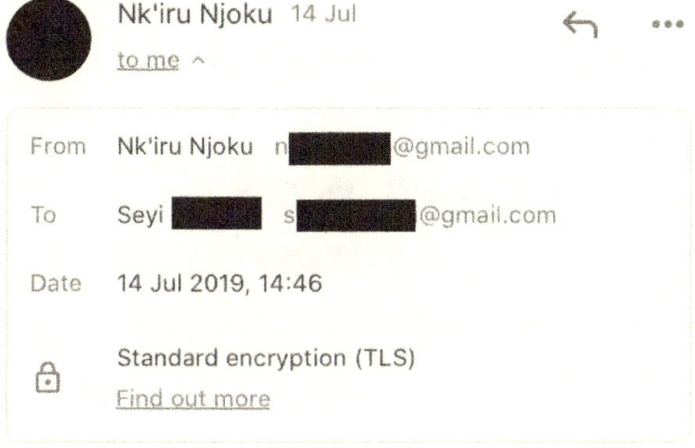

Okay cool. Let me know how it goes.

Listen, if none of this works, we have to take drastic measures, Seyi. I hope you know this? We are not going to sit down a few more days weighing our hands and leaving you in danger. Understand this please.

--

--

Nk'iru. Njoku

*wringing

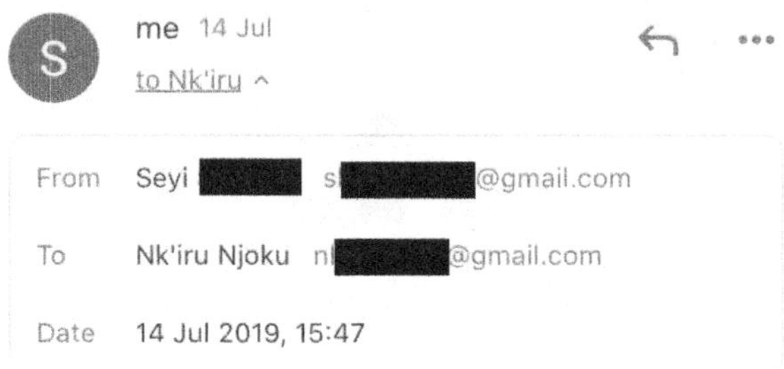

I understand

I lied. I understood nothing.

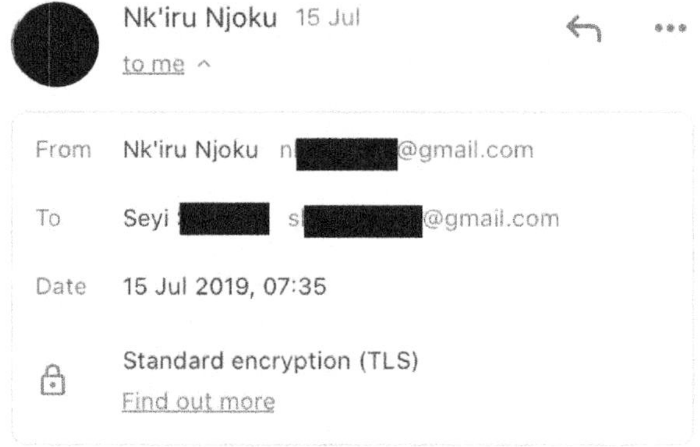

Hi Seyi.

What's the status of things?
--

--

Nk'iru. Njoku

I didn't get a chance to check and reply to my emails at the Afroprom event. Later that night, when we returned home, he started to ask me again if I wanted to leave him. I said no.

'Just let me know and I promise, I'll pack my things and walk out of the house.'

I believed him. I considered telling him, 'Yes. Just go.' But I stayed quiet.

'I just want to know where we stand.'

'Where will you live if you go?'

He shrugged. 'I'll sleep at my shop at night and leave in the morning.'

I knew this was hardly possible. His shop was in a building his father owned — the same building where his older sister lived.

At the same time, I was tired of lying.

'So do you want me to leave?' he asked again.

'Maybe,' I whispered.

'I'll take that as a yes,' he said.

As he walked away, I felt some relief and hoped he would pack his bags and leave.

He didn't.

He went downstairs, sat on the chair under the staircase, and began twisting his hair, frantically. A big, intense frown sat on his face. I had never seen him like this. I became terrified — I knew his strange behaviour did not portend any good. So, I joined him on the chair and told him that I wanted him to stay so we could work things out. He didn't seem entirely appeased, but the frown relaxed, somewhat.

I was mentally and emotionally exhausted; I wanted to go to bed. One of the girls had gotten into trouble and was on her knees, downstairs. Blessing was cleaning the kitchen.

'When Blessing is done, you can go too,' I said to the girl on her knees, and went upstairs.

My stomach began to hurt terribly. I hadn't been eating well since the July 8th incident and my ulcer had reared its painfully ugly head.

I was seated in the other room when he came around. I told him my stomach was hurting, and he offered to make me oats. He brought the oats, minutes later. I thought about this act of kindness and began to change my mind about leaving.

When he handed me the tray containing the oats, he stood, waiting for me to eat it.

I had the first spoon. It had an unpleasant taste and I was unable to eat it. I asked for more sugar and milk, which I added to the oats, but it didn't make it taste any better.

'Why does it taste so bad?' I asked him.

He blamed it on the maple sugar flavour in the oats, which did not make sense to me; but I had no better explanation, so it had to suffice. After a few more spoons, I stopped eating it; I just couldn't stomach the awful taste. He tried to get me to eat some more but I refused. He did not push. I had barely managed to lie down when I drifted off into a light sleep.

A little while later, I opened my eyes and found him standing and staring at me in the dark. I screamed and got off the bed. He quickly came to my side.

'I didn't mean to scare you. I just wanted to make sure you were fine.'

I knew the look I saw on his face when I opened my eyes and it wasn't that of concern. My heartbeat raced. Did he mean to poison me with the oats? Was he standing by watching if I would pass on from my sleep? Did he try to hurt me while I slept? As these questions romanced my mind, I knew for a fact that I needed to run from this man. I decided that, come morning, I would tell him I was leaving, since he had decided not to go for the meeting.

*

Monday morning dawned, and I watched the children get ready for school. I escorted them to the gate like I always did, and told the older kids, 'Stay in school when you close. I'll come pick you myself.'

I checked my email before heading inside. Nkiru's email was awaiting your reply.

Good morning.
Things are fine. I'm not sure he has plans of leaving the house today but I'll leave either ways.
I will speak with him when it's time to leave. He has been calm so far, He will be reasonable.
And I believe he is reluctant to leave the house because he has a feeling.
There will be no need for anything drastic I believe. The kids have gone to school. I can pick them up from school.
I suggested to talk to his sister and tell her what is happening so they can at least help him sort whatever issues he is having. He says no.

But from 12 noon or 1pm, I should be ready to leave.

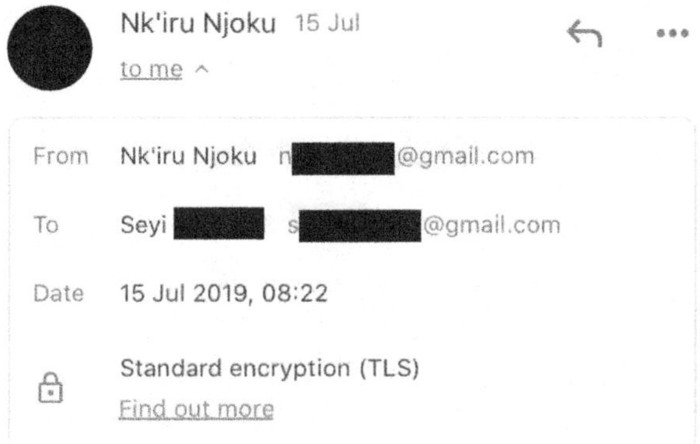

What makes you think he will let you leave the house on your own?

And if you speak to him as you say, does that not endanger you?

I'm worried.
--

--

Nk'iru. Njoku

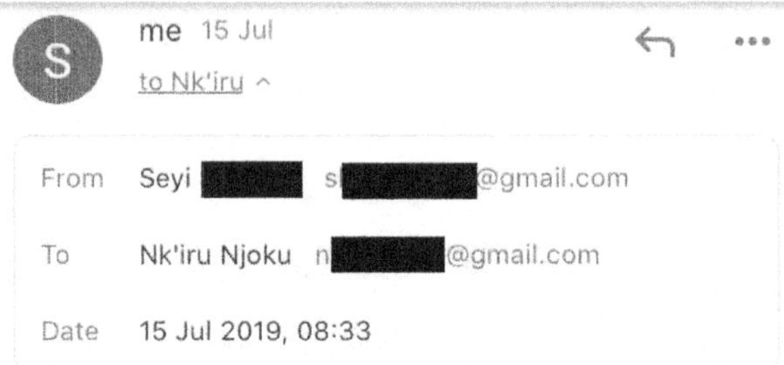

No. He really just had a crazy day that day.
I know I'm sounding unreasonable but It's the truth.
He will let me leave if I speak with him. He is not a terrible person. He just has issues of his own that he never tries to deal with.
I know the shirt guy called him. He said he will call back. I was there.
Also, I got his sister to try to get him out of the house. I'm just saying in case he doesn't leave.

But I promise, on this one- it will be fine. He won't hurt me.
I know I still sound crazy like a well groomed victim. I'm serious sha.

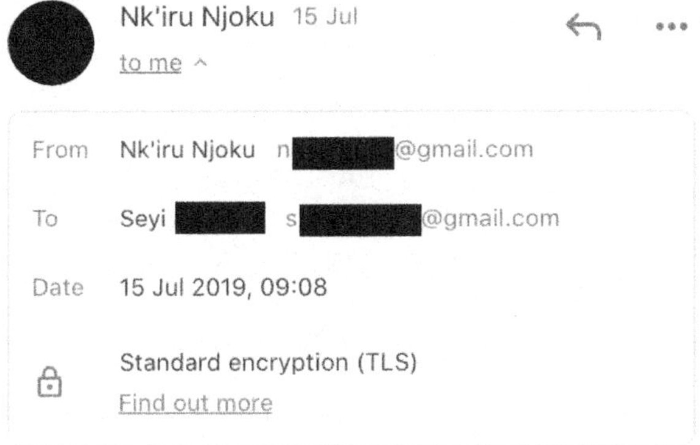

Nk'iru Njoku 15 Jul
to me

From	Nk'iru Njoku n████████@gmail.com
To	Seyi ████ s████████@gmail.com
Date	15 Jul 2019, 09:08
🔒	Standard encryption (TLS) Find out more

Seyi.

Understand a few things.

1. Yes, he has lured you into a sense of security that is totally FALSE.

2. He was not just 'having a bad day'. He has endangered you more than once. That isn't 'just having a bad day'.

3. This calm that you think exists? This is the calm before the storm. If you speak to him about leaving, he will turn on you so fiercely it will shock you.

4. Seyi, remember when he was going to snuff the life out of you and you saw no sympathy in his eyes? HE WAS NOT HAVING A BAD DAY.

5. When people are having a bad day, they get snappy, quiet, easily offended, etc. THEY DO NOT ALMOST KILL THEIR SPOUSE.

Now, here's what we want you to do.

DO NOT SPEAK TO HIM ABOUT LEAVING.

DO NOT TRY TO REASON WITH HIM. Remember that this safety you feel right now is FALSE. He is watching your every move. Watching your reactions. And the only way he can make you feel safe is by acting normal, JUST THE SAME WAY YOU HAVE BEEN ACTING NORMAL EVEN THOUGH YOU HAVE A PLAN.

Seyi, YOU DO NOT HAVE A HANDLE on this situation. Please stop thinking that your permutations are definitely correct.

We care more about you than about how he feels.

YOU ARE OUR PRIMARY CONCERN. YOU AND THE KIDS.

And we need to get you out of that house TODAY.

Remember: DO NOT TALK TO HIM ABOUT LEAVING. HIS RECENT BEHAVIOUR (which happened more than once!) IS ENOUGH TO SHOW US THAT THIS CALM IS FALSE.

Just stay quiet and 'normal' and we will continue to talk and plan how to get you out of there today.

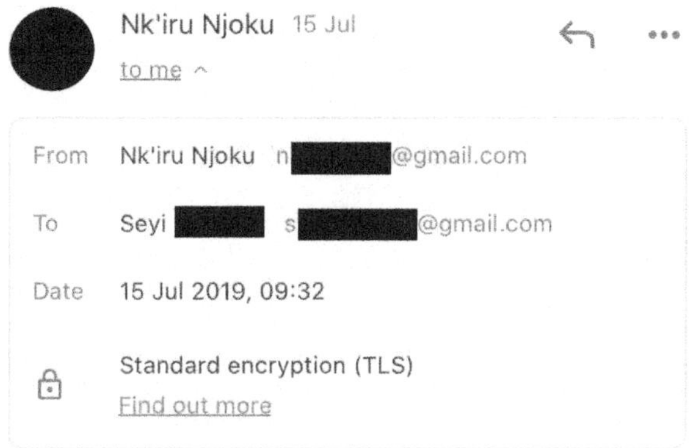

Seyi, what excuse can you use to leave the house for a few minutes? You don't need to pack anything for now, I mean just an excuse to come outside. How can you swing that?

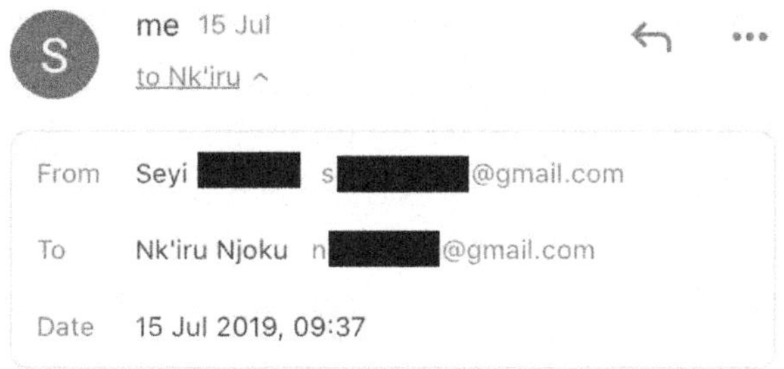

Okay.
I won't say anything to him about leaving.
I think he agreed to the meeting.
Do I get to carry my generator?

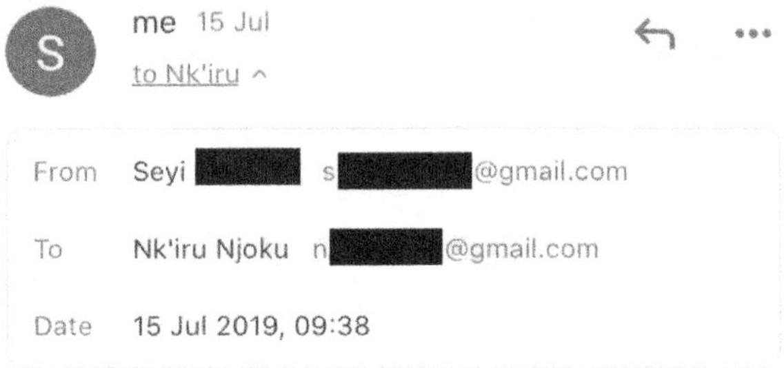

Ah, I don't know o. I am in the house with 3 kids too. Who didn't go to school.
But there is really no excuse. That I can think of.
Is there someone outside now?

Later that morning, inside the house, he started the conversation about making our marriage work again and promised to do better. He questioned me about where I stood, repeatedly; he knew I wasn't good at lying, and that I always gave in when I got tired of being drilled. What he did not know was that I was now fighting for my life; I couldn't afford to be my usual truthful self. I couldn't let my heart think for me, as it had led me to wrong places.

I convinced him that I was ready to make it work, even as I convinced him to go for the meeting. I reminded him we could use some extra money in the house.

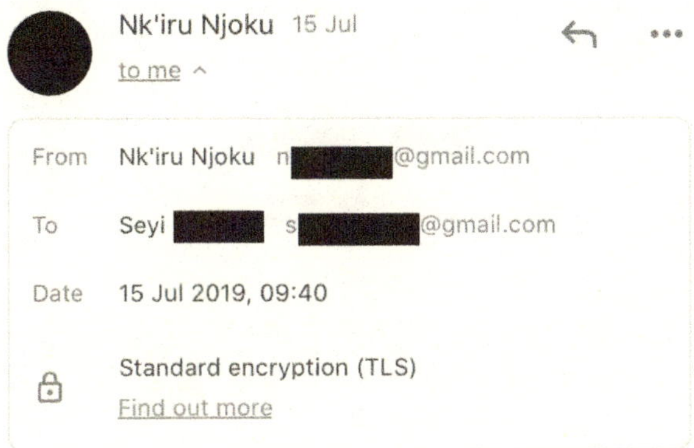

No, not now.

We meant if he doesn't go out. I had sent that email before seeing your response to the initial one.

So what time is he going to go out?
--

--

Nk'iru. Njoku

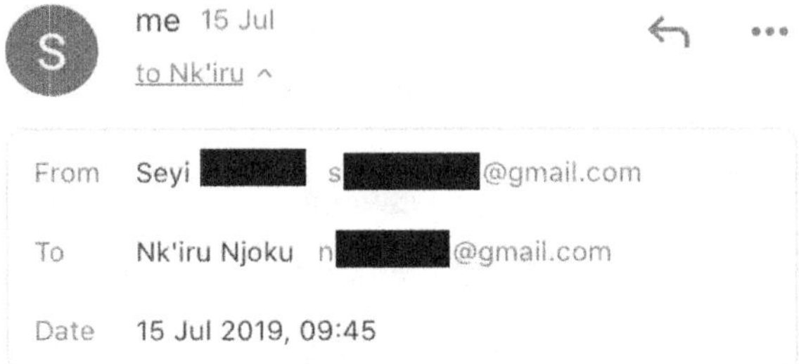

They planned the meeting for 12.
He should leave at about 11 or 11:30 although he keeps saying there is something about the meeting that isn't right.
He says he will still go though because we need the money.
But I suggest that we confirm he is at the meeting or at least maybe 30minutes to an hour after he has left the house. Once he leaves I will start moving stuff around as much as I can.
It's just basic items especially for the kids.
So that once there vehicle is around, we move in the space of 5-10 minutes and go over to the schools.
Two different schools - primary and secondary

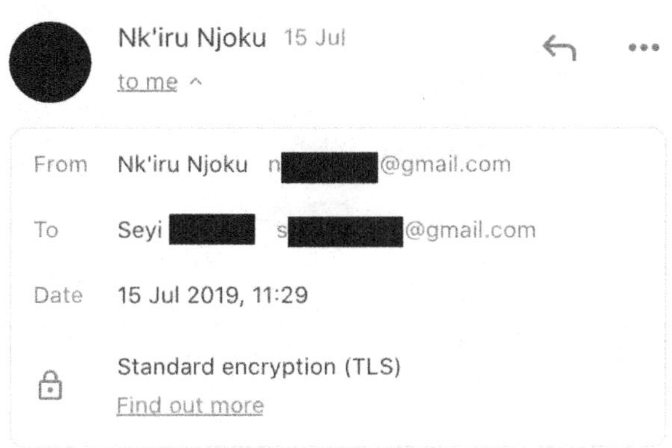

Nk'iru Njoku 15 Jul
to me

From	Nk'iru Njoku	n█████@gmail.com
To	Seyi █████	s█████@gmail.com
Date	15 Jul 2019, 11:29
🔒	Standard encryption (TLS) Find out more

Has he gone out?
--

--

Nk'iru. Njoku

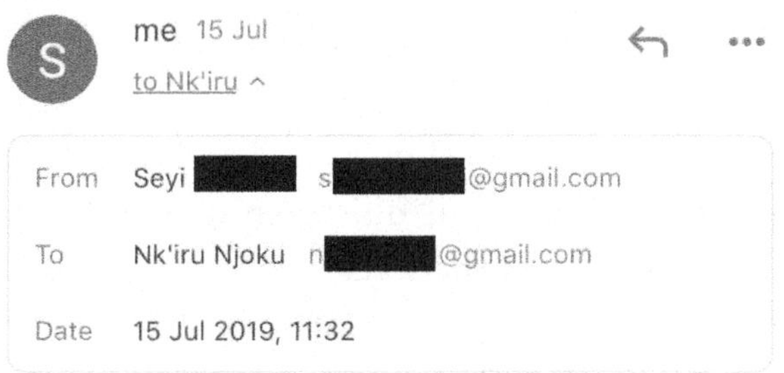

me 15 Jul
to Nk'iru

From	Seyi █████	s█████@gmail.com
To	Nk'iru Njoku	n█████@gmail.com
Date	15 Jul 2019, 11:32

About to. In like 5 minutes

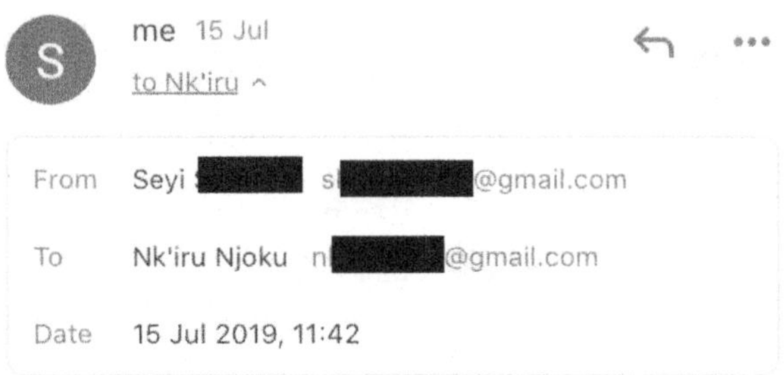

He has gone out.
I'm confused. What do I pack? Apart from the kids clothes and dance costumes.

As soon as he left the house, I retrieved the children's phone from Blessing, turned it off and asked her to pack a few things for the kids in a bag. She was reluctant but I hastened her.

I would find out days later that he had told Blessing to call him if I ever tried to leave the house. I had been a step ahead by collecting the phone from her before making any move.

I looked at the list of things I had made earlier to know what to pack, but I still didn't know where to start. I started to shiver and then, tears followed. I realised that I really didn't want to go. Maybe he had truly made a mistake. While I had now become convinced that we would resolve our issues, I decided to leave the house first.

I checked my email.

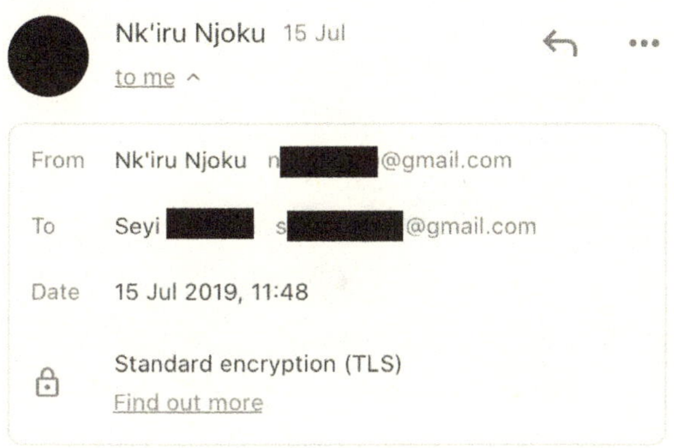

Your passport and any important document.
Ijeoma is already in your estate.
--

--

Nk'iru. Njoku

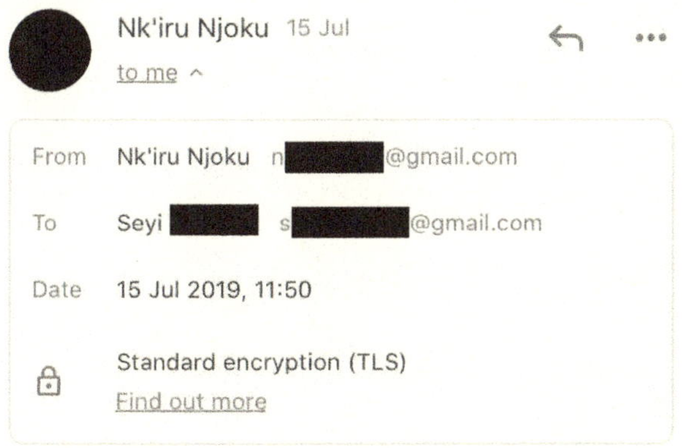

When can ijeoma call you?

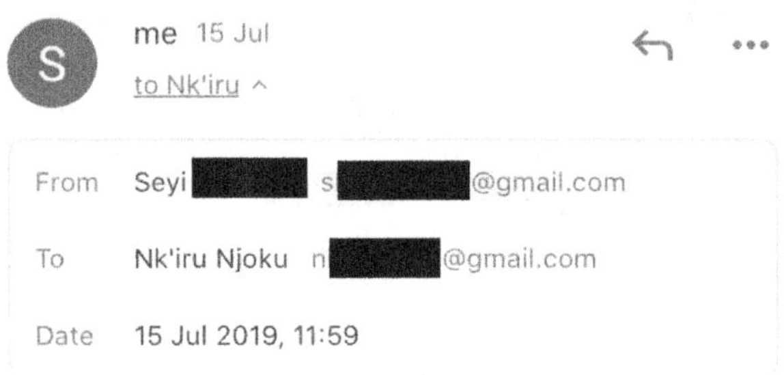

Okay. 10 minutes maybe.

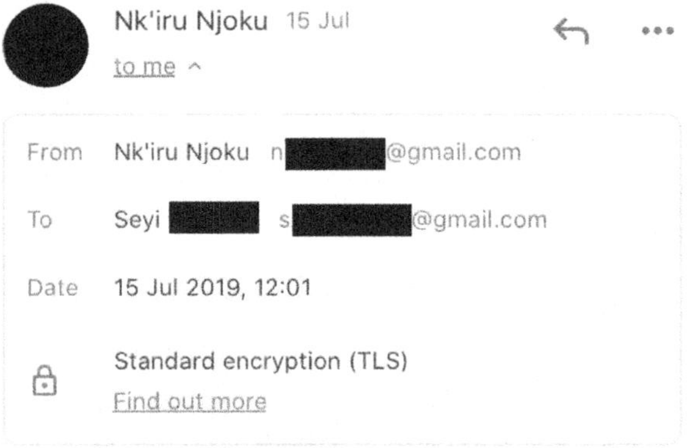

You can take your gen if you want. As long as we are sure he has really left and he's not hanging around and watching the house.

But documents and laptop first!
--

--

Nk'iru. Njoku

I packed my documents, including my passport and the kids' passports. I had his passport with me, so I dropped it in the wardrobe. I saw the Dream Catchers' complimentary card; I wanted to take it, but I believed I would be back home soon, so I left it. We just needed to fix this.

I took my wedding certificate; Nkiru and my sister had told me to always make sure this document was in my possession.

I had made part payment on a property I put both our names on, and when I saw the documents to the property, I knew I was meant to take them with me. Yet, I decided to leave them, believing that once he noticed I left them, he would realise that I still had some faith in this marriage.

Then, I took a Post-it Note and wrote, 'I love you. You need to get help.'

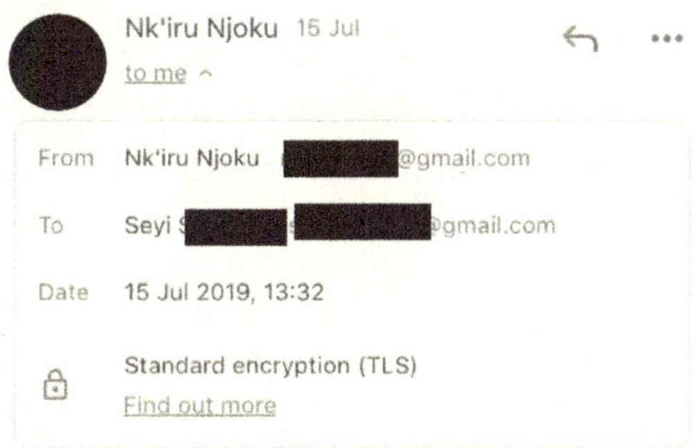

By the time I was done packing, I got a call from Ijeoma, asking if I was ready. I said yes.

She came into the house and asked me to hurry; we couldn't risk him coming back and finding us. At that point, I believed she was overreacting just like everyone else, but I tried to hurry.

I left with my few packed items, Blessing, and the two younger girls; then, we headed to the kids' schools to pick them up. They were confused and wanted to know where we were going. I told them we were taking a short trip.

With my kids safely with me, Ijeoma said I had to write a police report. I shook my head. There was no way I was writing a report against the love of my life; my husband. She told me how important it was and insisted that it was necessary to prevent him from claiming that I was kidnapped. When we got to the police station, I didn't know what to write in my statement. I didn't want him arrested.

I would regret this decision days and months later.

I penned down an incoherent sentence, paid ₦2,000 for the case to be filed, and left the station.

CHAPTER EIGHT

THE STORM

"In order to escape accountability for his crimes, the perpetrator does everything in his power to promote forgetting. If secrecy fails, the perpetrator attacks the credibility of his victim. If he cannot silence her absolutely, he tries to make sure no one listens."
— Judith Lewis Herman

After I left the police station, I texted my sister and told her not to stop by the house that day. She would normally show up on Mondays to spend the night so that she could attend her fellowship, which was close to our house, the next morning.

When she asked why, I told her that my husband had tried to kill me, so I had to run away. I waited for her to quote a scripture encouraging me to pray away his bad behaviour; instead, she was shocked. She wanted to know where I was and if I was okay. I was relieved to have her on my side. I let her know I was in a rescue van heading somewhere I was not sure about yet.

During the drive, I wept profusely. Ijeoma continued to assure me that I'd be fine, and that this was probably the end of the marriage. I did not agree or believe her. I was convinced something would eventually give. I believed that when his mother heard the story, she would be very angry with him and make him apologise and promise to be better. I was not sure what exactly would lead me back to the house, but I felt like it was not over. The situation would be resolved.

I was taken to a hide out. I couldn't get myself out of that place if I wanted to. Ijeoma assured me that I would be safe there and he wouldn't be able to find me. After showing us around the house, she announced that she had to take her leave; then, she gave me a big, tight hug that made me cry.

When I was alone, I wept. I started to remember how apologetic he was. I imagined that he would finally give me the grand gesture I had always wanted from him. I was sure he would come home with a big cake, the pink panther doll I had always wanted from Miniso, and some fresh roses. I started to feel sad as I imagined how broken he would be to see that I was not home.

I worried and wondered how he would consume all the cake, whom he would give my gifts to. I scolded myself for listening to Nkiru and leaving the house. He was finally going to give me what I'd always wanted and I wasn't going to be home to receive it. I wished I could run back home, so he would meet me when he got back and shower me with love and gifts.

At about 4 p.m., my phone rang — it was him. I began to shiver; I could feel an anxiety attack coming on. My stomach had started to hurt too, but I did not answer his calls. He sent me a series of WhatsApp messages, but they were not the apologies and pleas I had been expecting. Instead, they were threats and manipulative messages; messages where he distorted the chain of events and blamed me for all that had happened.

He also sent me a picture of a ₦2,500 Miniso cup saying, 'See what I bought for you.' On seeing the picture of the cup, the scales fell off my eyes. HE BOUGHT ME A CUP? He tried to kill me and decided the best way to placate me was by buying me a cup? A cup that I could have walked into Miniso to buy at any time that I wanted? I literally had just bought a new cup before the incident. He couldn't go all out to show how sorry he was?

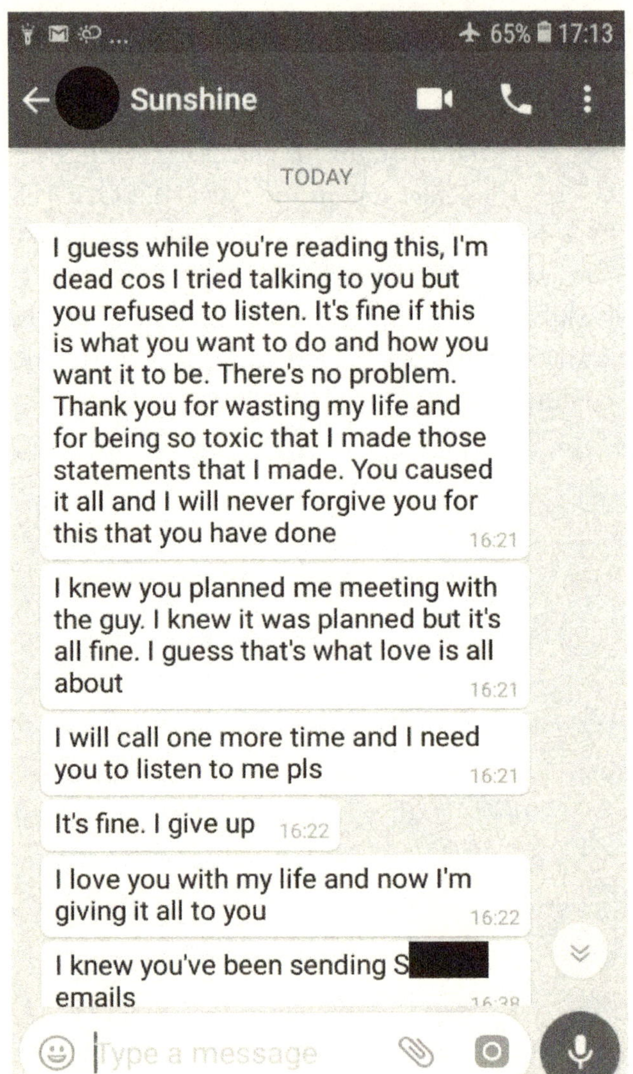
Sunshine

TODAY

I guess while you're reading this, I'm dead cos I tried talking to you but you refused to listen. It's fine if this is what you want to do and how you want it to be. There's no problem. Thank you for wasting my life and for being so toxic that I made those statements that I made. You caused it all and I will never forgive you for this that you have done
16:21

I knew you planned me meeting with the guy. I knew it was planned but it's all fine. I guess that's what love is all about
16:21

I will call one more time and I need you to listen to me pls
16:21

It's fine. I give up
16:22

I love you with my life and now I'm giving it all to you
16:22

I knew you've been sending S███ emails
16:38

Type a message

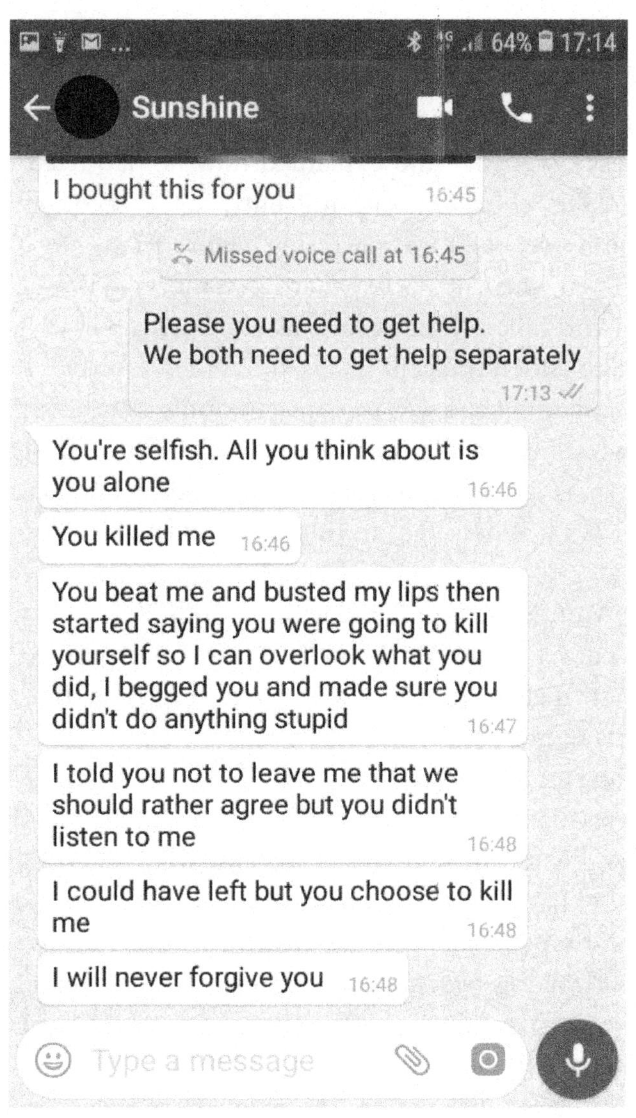

I was highly pained and disappointed.

At this point, I remembered that I hadn't informed any of his family members about the situation. I felt the need to tell them since they had been so nice to me. I called his eldest sister first and explained how he had tried to kill me. She chuckled intermittently as I recounted my experience, like I was narrating a childish event.

Then, she said, 'Sorry. I am in a meeting now. I'll call him and talk to him as soon as I am done. Sorry.'

She ended the call.

I assumed she was too busy to understand the gravity of what her brother had done. I called his second sister, who was in the United States and repeated my narration of events. When I got to the Sniper part, she interrupted me.

'Wait, wait. Where is the Sniper now?'

'I don't know. Maybe in the house,' I responded.

'Ah. Let me call him and make sure he is fine. I will come back to you.'

She ended the call.

At this moment, I was not sure how I felt, exactly.

A few minutes later, his second sister called me back to say that he was not answering her call and asked that I call him to make sure he was okay. I don't know what I was thinking but I actually agreed. I called his number twice but it didn't go through, and in retrospect, I am grateful for this.

My sister insisted on knowing where I was, so I gave her the address. Shortly after, she visited, asking to know all that happened. As soon as I narrated the course of events to her, her phone rang. He was the one calling. He told her I left the house after a mild argument, and that he knew I was with her.

'She is not with me,' I heard my sister say. 'You need to figure out the situation and let me know where she is.' She ended the call.

I was terrified. We contemplated on whom to tell first and decided on my eldest brother. On hearing what had happened, he was infuriated, cursing loudly on the phone. Then, I called my father and narrated the same course of events to him. He asked to know where I was, but I refused to divulge that information. I just let him know that I was doing fine.

I told my sister that I suspected Blessing's loyalty had been compromised, but I needed to get her story before it changed. So, I had my sister do a video recording of Blessing recounting what she witnessed on the 8th of July, 2019.

Finally, we called my mum. Her reaction was startlingly different and unexpected. Apparently, Toba had gotten to her before me, and told her his version of things. By the time I recounted how I experienced the past few days, it was difficult to tell if she was on my side. It didn't seem like she was, and I felt like I needed everyone on my side.

My sister left a few hours after we were served *eba* and soup by our host. I couldn't eat.

I called his sister back and she told me she had been able to reach him. I asked if she had explained the situation to their mother.

'You call her yourself and explain. It's better,' she said.

I called his mother and explained all that had happened to her.

'Is that why you now left the house?' she asked me in Yoruba. 'And you know I am not around.'

'I said he tried to kill me ma,' I responded in Yoruba.

'God forbid that happens. Tomorrow, pack your bags with the kids and go back to the house.'

Unaccustomed to arguing with elders, I said, 'Okay.'

She went on to ask me to call his father to explain what I had just told her, to him. I told her I would do as she had said.

Then, I called my parents to let them know what his mother said, and to also let them know that I wouldn't be going back to the house.

*

I was still desperately hoping that someone would see what had happened, so I called his father. By the time I finished narrating the series of events to his father, he said he didn't believe me and he didn't believe his son either. He asked me to come to their house with Blessing and two of my foster sons so he could interrogate us all. When I told him I couldn't make it, he said he would call my parents, and ended the call.

I emailed Nkiru at every point, as the day progressed. She and Ijeoma continued to check in to be sure I was doing okay. I felt safe having these women in my life.

It got dark soon and everyone needed to sleep. I had three of the girls stay with me in the room because I was too scared to sleep alone. Still, I was unable to sleep.

I cried until there were no more tears to shed. I dozed off at intervals, but my fear awakened me each time. Then, I would look out the window to make sure he was not there in the dark, waiting to get me.

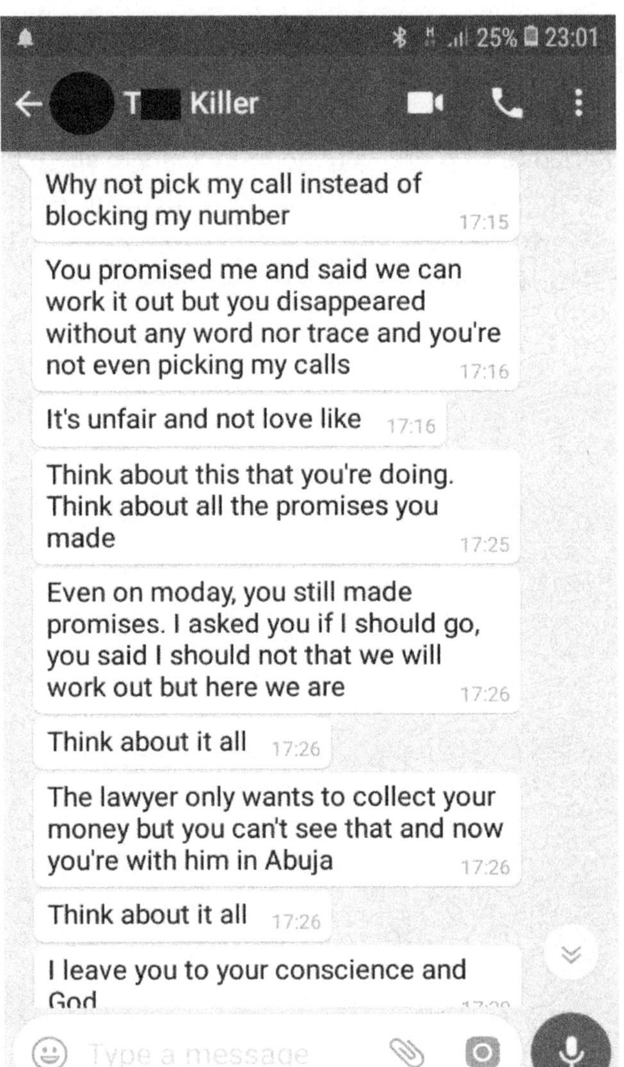
25% 23:01
T▮ Killer
Why not pick my call instead of
blocking my number
17:15
You promised me and said we can
work it out but you disappeared
without any word nor trace and you're
not even picking my calls
17:16
It's unfair and not love like
17:16
Think about this that you're doing.
Think about all the promises you
made
17:25
Even on moday, you still made
promises. I asked you if I should go,
you said I should not that we will
work out but here we are
17:26
Think about it all
17:26
The lawyer only wants to collect your
money but you can't see that and now
you're with him in Abuja
17:26
Think about it all
17:26
I leave you to your conscience and
God
17:29
Type a message

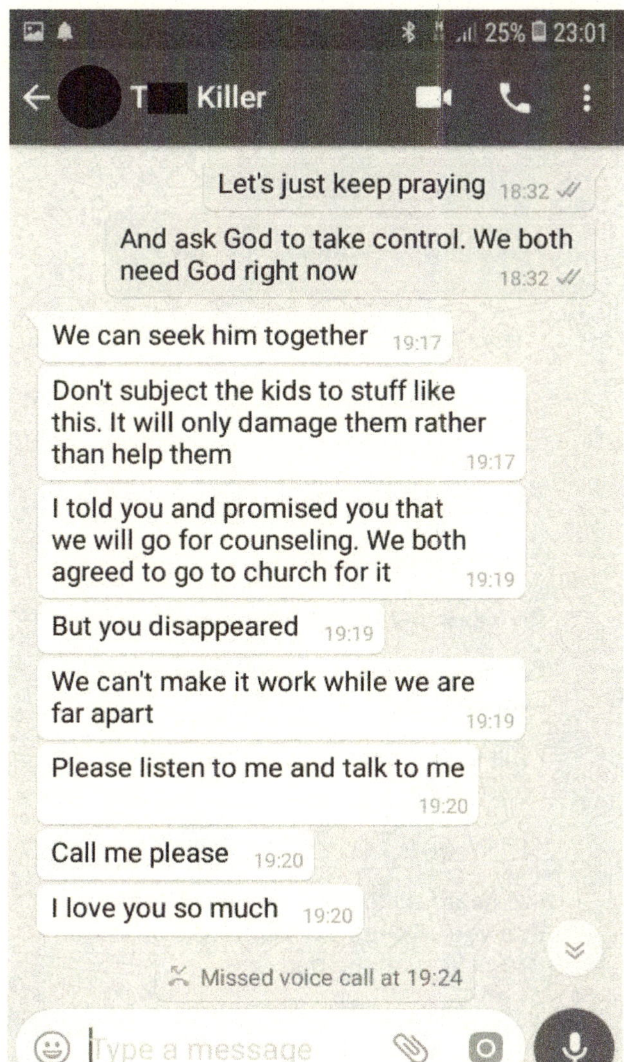

25% 23:01
T███ Killer
Let's just keep praying 18:32
And ask God to take control. We both need God right now 18:32
We can seek him together 19:17
Don't subject the kids to stuff like this. It will only damage them rather than help them 19:17
I told you and promised you that we will go for counseling. We both agreed to go to church for it 19:19
But you disappeared 19:19
We can't make it work while we are far apart 19:19
Please listen to me and talk to me 19:20
Call me please 19:20
I love you so much 19:20
Missed voice call at 19:24
Type a message

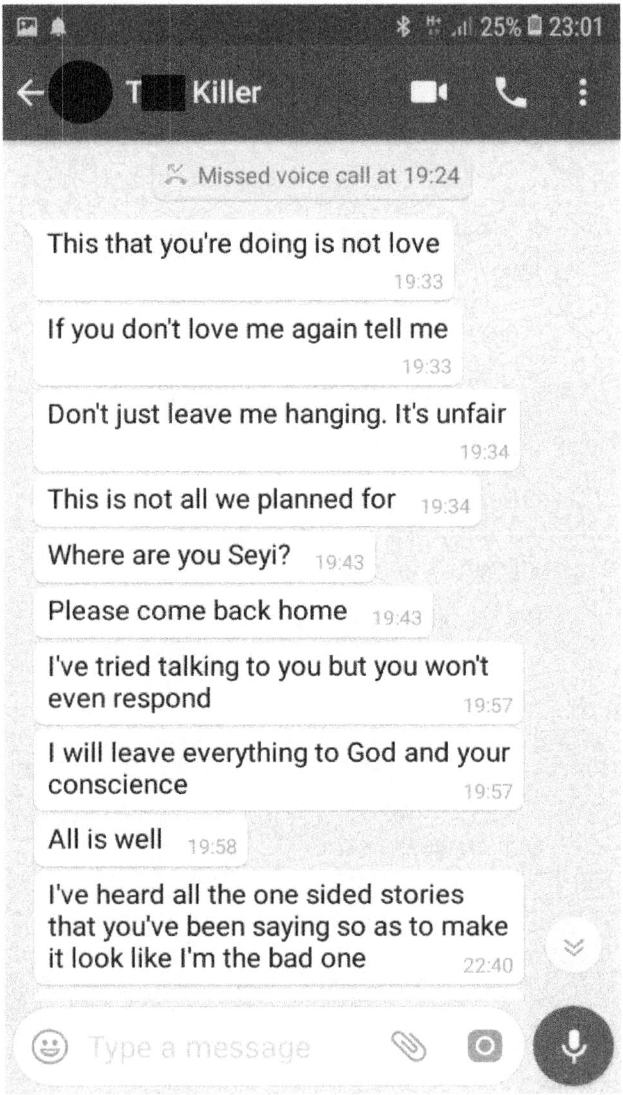

T▮▮ Killer

Missed voice call at 19:24

This that you're doing is not love
19:33

If you don't love me again tell me
19:33

Don't just leave me hanging. It's unfair
19:34

This is not all we planned for 19:34

Where are you Seyi? 19:43

Please come back home 19:43

I've tried talking to you but you won't
even respond
19:57

I will leave everything to God and your
conscience
19:57

All is well 19:58

I've heard all the one sided stories
that you've been saying so as to make
it look like I'm the bad one
22:40

Type a message

CHAPTER NINE

BLESSING OR CURSE?

"Stab the body and it heals, but injure the heart and the wound lasts a lifetime."
— Mineko Iwasaki

Dawn broke with a torrent of rain pouring from the sky. For a moment, I wished the rain would wash away my memory and all this bad luck.

I looked out the window to confirm that he hadn't found me. I was still scared. My stomach rumbled and I rushed to use the toilet. While on the toilet seat, I remembered the events of the past few days and I decided on my next line of action once I stepped out.

First thing I did was summon Blessing and ask her what relationship she had with my husband.

She started by beating about the bush, saying nothing and saying a lot at the same time. I reminded her of all the good I had done for her; how I had loved and cared for her since she was 14, when she almost dropped out of school. She maintained that they never had a relationship.

I realised that this 19-year-old before me was now a stranger. Then, I adopted a different approach, reminding her of how my husband had brought a bottle of Sniper into the room to kill me. I reminded her that she was right behind the door when he entered the room with the Sniper; I let her know I heard her voice.

I gave her another chance at redemption. 'Tell me now or I will add your name to the police report as an accomplice to my attempted murder,' I told her.

The mention of the police scared her.

'I told him not to take the Sniper inside the room but he said did I remember the day I gave you palm oil because you swallowed medicine. He said he only wants to help you with the Sniper,' she said.

I asked her how she thought he was trying to save me by bringing in Sniper to the room where I was. My hurt deepened as I questioned Blessing — here was a girl I trusted with my life.

'Tell me all the truth, Blessing,' I demanded, again.

She faked a sob and told me how he was the one who would always wake her up every midnight to talk to her. She said he would ask her to hug him and she would run away. She talked about how he would call her and how she would always tell him, 'Stop calling me. I am not your wife.'

Her stories were all over the place. Yet, I had just one question for her. 'Why did you never tell me? Even all those times I asked you if anything was going on.'

I wanted Blessing to be open to me because I had every intention of following through with her case. I didn't want to send her home. For some reason, I still felt some responsibility towards helping her.

But she refused to tell the truth, only hinting at minute details that barely made sense. Eventually, she said he had asked her to be his girlfriend because I was already old, but that she turned down his advances. She also told me how he always wrote letters to her but took them back once she had read them, and how he deleted the messages on her phone every time they met. She told me how he had touched her breast and opened her shirt without her consent, and how she had run away from him that night. She told me how he threatened her not to tell anyone about him touching her, because if she did, he would deny it, and no one would believe her.

All at once, feelings of failure and betrayal consumed me. I felt like I had failed this young woman.

Maybe if I had asked her more often.

Maybe all those times when I suspected something and called her to ask if things were okay, maybe if I had asked her more than 10 times.

I had gotten her a counsellor and I asked why she never told the counsellor any of what she went through. She had no answers for me.

I asked her why she didn't hide any of the messages he sent and find a way to show it to me. I reminded her of the sex education and how I always told her that I would believe her, no matter who the perpetrator was.

As I spoke to her, one thing stood out strikingly to me: there was no remorse in her eyes. She made crying sounds but there were no tears. Her loyalty was no longer to me. Despite my telling her that he had no money and I was the one who had been fending for him, myself and all the kids, she didn't seem to care.

As I wrote this chapter, I listened to the voice recording I made of Blessing when I tried to get her to tell me the truth, and I realised how much he had manipulated and brainwashed her - so much so, she never trusted me enough to tell me what really transpired between them. From the first time he called her away and said he wanted to help her, she should have come to me. People have told me that he was manipulative and that he used her. I understand that. But hers was a disaster that could have been avoided.

I never trusted him; it was her that I trusted. I trusted her so much that every time I suspected their affair and I asked, once she said there was nothing, I believed her. Every single time.

*

It had been 24 hours since we left the house, and in all that time he never stopped calling me. I shivered each time I saw his name on my caller ID. For every time I blocked him, I unblocked him. I couldn't find the strength to block him permanently, and I didn't have the courage to pick his call.

My foster kids were curious as to why we left our house. They had no clothes and no underwear — they wore their school uniforms throughout. I had asked Blessing to pack their bags, and it seemed she had packed all the unnecessary things, on purpose, so that we'd have cause to go back to the house.

'Maama, what happened?' Dami asked, cornering me outside the safe house.

'Call Semilore and Shola for me first,' I said. Those were my two teenage boys. I wanted to tell them first. I didn't want them to put any woman through what I was going through.

I could barely get a full sentence out of my mouth as I tried to explain why we had to leave the house, without crying. I could see the shock and confusion on Semilore's face. Shola's eyes were filled with mostly anger.

As I explained, I would burst into tears intermittently. 'Sorry ma,' they would say, each time.

'No wonder every time we are reading he used to say Sister Blessing should stay behind so he can teach her more,' Shola said.

Semilore stayed quiet for a few seconds, then walked away. Shola followed him. Shola came back about two minutes later, still angry.

'I have told her to never come close to you again,' he said.

His loyalty warmed my heart, but I was also afraid. Afraid that if we alienated her, she'd find a way to bring him to us.

'Just be careful,' I admonished, but Shola's mind was made up. He insisted that they would never have anything to do with her.

The boys told the younger girls about Blessing's behavior and they immediately ceased all forms of association with her.

Everyone advised that I let Blessing go. Her presence in my life was dangerous. Her loyalty was no longer to me and she could find a way to contact him.

I heard and understood the counsel, but I didn't want to take it. I kept her around me. I wanted to see her through secondary school. I was worried she wouldn't get enough time to study or achieve anything if I sent her back to her struggling mother.

I kept her around for about three more days, until she started to taunt me.

Every hour, she'd call me aside to give me some flimsy detail about her relationship with my husband. One hour, she was telling me about the times he'd give her money and the next hour, she was telling me about how he complained she was being slow to accept his advances. Every time she called me aside to tell me another detail, my heart sank.

I wasn't sure why she was telling me those things. Then one day, she told me about the time my husband had asked her to spy on me because according to him, I was cheating and had gone to see my lover. I decided I couldn't take it anymore.

I called her mother and explained what her daughter had done.

'Blessing *ti baye je!*' her mother exclaimed over the phone. *Blessing has spoilt the world!*

A few hours later, I called her to the same corner she had been calling me to tell me those flimsy details. 'I am taking you back to your mother,' I said.

'Please ma,' she begged with those empty eyes.

'You will only be there for a few days,' I lied, so that her tears wouldn't guilt me into letting her stay.

She begged that I reconsider my decision but I didn't budge.

I took her to her mother.

When her mother saw her, she avoided her gaze. Blessing did the same. Her mother asked her similar questions to the ones I had asked, but she insisted nothing was going on between her and my husband. She remained unrepentant, and her eyes stayed empty.

I reminded her mother of the promise I made to see Blessing through secondary school. I told her I intended to keep true to my word and asked that she let me know details required for Blessing to register for and write her exams.

I still run into Blessing at my parents' house, occasionally. She has never apologised. Every time I see her, my heart skips and I feel the sudden onset of anxiety. The feeling of anger has subsided over the past months, but I'd rather not have to see her again.

One afternoon when I visited my parents, I saw her.

'Good afternoon ma,' she said.

'Never in your life should you open your mouth to greet me. Do you understand?'

She nodded and left.

People have told me that she is as much a victim as I am; that she was manipulated too, as there were power dynamics involved. I do not disagree. But this doesn't shrink my hurt and pain.

And what hurts the most, is that I did all I could for this young lady and she never came clean.

CHAPTER TEN

THE STRUGGLE

"It took me a long time to realize the difference between the people we are drawn to and the people who are good for us."
— **Steve Maraboli**

You'd think leaving an abusive relationship would be the most difficult part, but nobody and nothing can prepare you for the struggles that will come, once you make this decision. All of a sudden, everyone has an opinion and the pressure from every angle weighs more than the heaviest dumbbells.

I thought carrying my bags that afternoon and running out of that house with my foster kids would be the hardest part, after which life would go on as usual and things would go back to normal.

How wrong could I have been?

I had no clothes for the longest time. My foster kids had no clothes. I was dealing with ulcer pains and lack of appetite all at once. Despite the challenges I was facing, I had to keep working.

I remember that Beyoncé's album, Black is King, came out at this time and the girls danced to 'Brown Skin Girl' in their school underwear, tights, and odd clothes we found around the safe house. Some even had to wear singlets. I wept as I edited that dance video.

It was a lot.

After two weeks at my hideout, my sister offered that we move to her house. We did, and things became a little easier. I bought new clothes, shoes and underwear for my foster kids — their entire wardrobes, replaced.

The goal was to move on, move ahead, and never look back.

But he never stopped calling me. His mother would call. His sister would call. My mother would call. The pressure to return to my marital home was insane. I received countless calls and text messages, back to back, all day long. It felt like the more I tried to heal, the more my situation and reality sucked me back in to dance with ghosts from my past.

Every morning, I didn't know whose message or phone call I'd wake up to. His mother's? My mother's? His sister's? His?

One night, I wet the bed. I was 28 years old and I wet the bed. The same would happen to me as a 29-year-old after having a nightmare about my domestic violence experience.

It felt like my world was caving in, and I was fast losing sight of the future I sought.

I began to keep a journal to hang on to my sanity.

*

His mother called me once and said, 'Seyi, *ma sebi awon obirin* social media *to ma fi ile oko le, nitori won ti* popular.' *Do not be like those social media women who leave their husbands when they become famous.*

'Mummy, *mo ni omo yin fe pami.*' I reminded her that her son tried to kill me and hadn't stopped stalking me.

'*Ife ni. Oruko e nikan lonpe. Oni iwo ni Lavida. Mi o* expect *gbo gbo eleyi rara. Adura mi ni pe ki olorun bami fi omo gidi si arin yin.*' *It's love. He calls only your name and says you are his life. I did not expect these from you both. My prayer has been for you both to have a good child.*

'*Se pelu ise ti ko ni? Ka bimo tan, ka wa toro owo* Pampers?' I said to her. *He is jobless. Would we have a child and start begging for Pampers money all around?*

'*Olorun oni je,*' she responded. *God forbid.*

I only picked her calls out of respect. I hoped that one day she'd acknowledge that her son had wronged me, but that never happened. She trivialized my entire experience and only looked for ways to get me back with her murderous, mentally unstable son. I eventually stopped picking her calls.

I gradually came to the realisation that she would never apologise for what I had gone through or ever be on my side. It hurt, but I guess her loyalty is to her son.

*

He called all my friends, everyone he knew I had any form of relationship with. He told them that I ran off — that he loved me and he was sure I could not be fine without him. Knowing who I had married, I was already one step ahead of him. From the evening I left, even while nursing my heartbreak, I called all my friends and acquaintances to let them know what transpired.

One of my friends told me he would call her and say, 'I know Seyi is not fine without me. Tell me where she is.'

My friend and Colleague, *J*, told me that Toba called him, and he'd had to warn him to leave me alone.

He sent DMs and inbox messages on social media; it was exhausting having people tell me every other day that he had called or messaged them.

Nkiru sent me an email to say he had sent her messages on Facebook, asking for the next story workshop we would be having because he wanted to surprise me. He obviously had no idea Nkiru knew about what had happened.

A year later, when I went to the hotel we used for our writing workshops, one of the attendants told me that he had visited the hotel with our wedding album, insisting that he wanted to know my room number to surprise me. The attendant said he told him I wasn't in the hotel, but he sat at the reception all day. He didn't leave until he was sure I wasn't there.

*

He did everything he could to get me to come back. Barely 48 hours after I left, his sister deactivated the PayPal and GoFundMe accounts she had been running for my non-profit; then, he told me he could get her to reactivate the accounts if I came home.

He logged into one of my work Gmail accounts and deleted an interview invitation while I was reading it! It seemed surreal to me the day it happened. He didn't stop there. He went into the account, changed the recovery email address and recovery number, then, deleted the existence of the email.

When I confronted him, he insisted he knew nothing about it but once I was able to recover the account, I saw his details on the account.

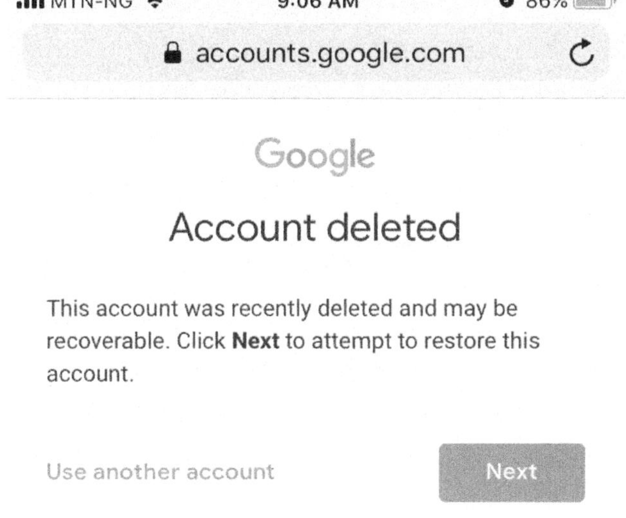

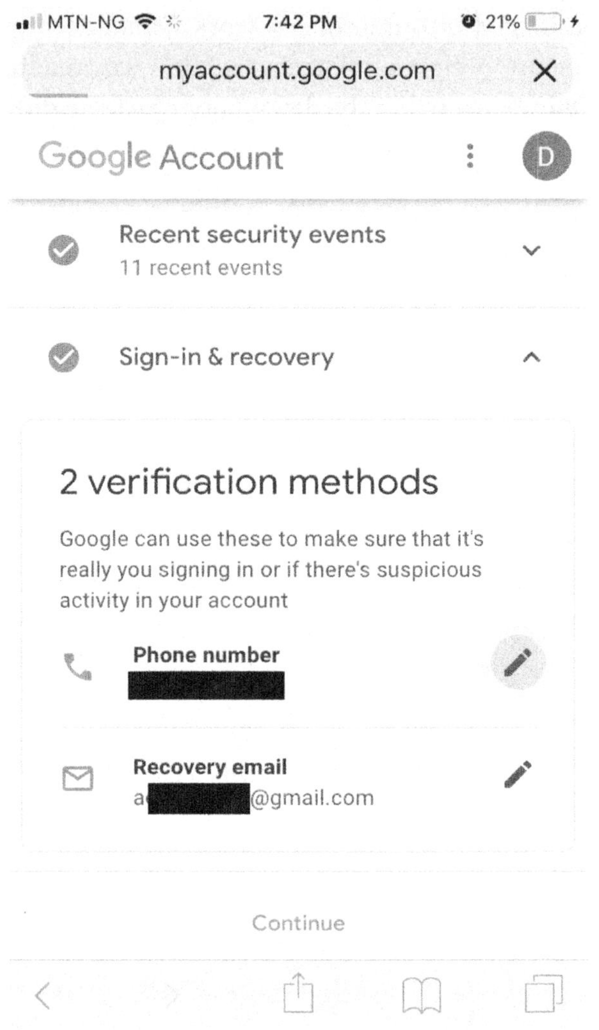

He hijacked the website he had helped build for my organisation and my personal brand. He changed the password and strengthened the firewall, to the point that

even hackers were finding it difficult to take down the
site.

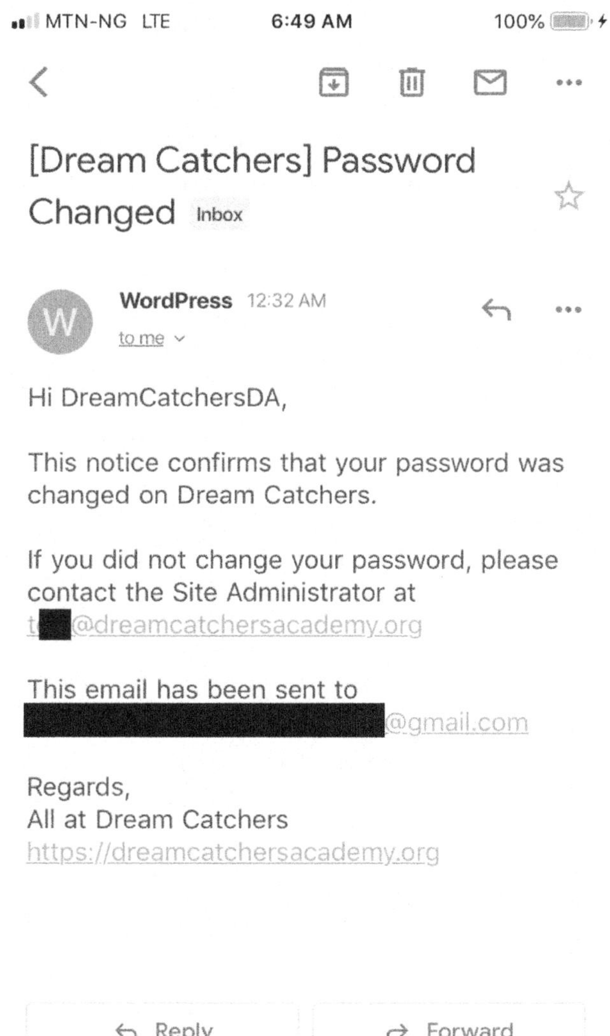

*

The pressure was intense; I was convinced I would lose my mind. Everyone advised that I relocate or make some drastic changes to allow me adjust to the new normal or at least move on. I agreed, but I didn't have these options. I didn't have the funds and I wasn't about to leave my foster kids behind.

To get some time away, I took all the money in my savings, booked a hotel, and decided I'd stay there for a weekend to clear my head.

On the Friday of my weekend getaway, he badgered my phone with messages, that I threw my phone against a wall in sheer frustration.

The next day, a Saturday, I got a call from my long-time family friend, Deborah, whom I now call my cousin. She knew all that had been happening, and told me about a dream she had. In the dream, my abusive ex-husband came begging. I listened and went back with him, only for him to wait a few years later to exact his revenge on me. She begged me not to go back to him.

'Aunty Seyi, no matter what happens, don't go back. He will kill you,' she said.

I thanked her for the call and promised to stay strong.

My foster girls would usually have a ballet dance class at Lekki every Saturday. He used to come with us, and I suspected that he would come around, so I told the girls to go without me. After a few hours, I confirmed from the volunteer who accompanied them if he came by. She said he did not.

I was missing my kids and I wanted to see them again so I decided to show up at the studio. I chose an outfit that made me feel sexy and confident.

I was in the waiting room, taking pictures and *gisting* with my younger cousin when I felt someone's hands touch me. I looked to my side and it was him. I screamed as hard as I could, yelling at him to leave me.

His grip was tight as he repeated the words, 'I am sorry.' I saw the devil in his eyes, not remorse.

I screamed and begged that he leave me alone. My cousin regarded us quietly, in shock. Two attendants at the studio came in and saw me screaming, and him on his knees, his hands still gripping me tightly. I hoped they'd interfere and ask him to leave, but they left after a few seconds of watching the scene unfold.

Eventually, he released me from his grip but refused to leave. He begged and asked that I follow him back home.

'I want to speak with you. I want to tell you something.'

'I am listening,' I responded, in fear.

'Tell Amen to leave the room.'

My cousin chuckled and said, 'I am not going anywhere.'

'Seyi, see the way Amen is talking to me anyhow,' he said. I could see the familiar anger in his eyes.

'Say what you want to say. She is not going.' I struggled to sound confident in the midst of fear that beclouded my mind.

'I'll tell you what happened with Blessing. Just tell her to leave.'

I shook my head.

He started making his usual promises of being a better husband. He continued to apologise and although I could see the devilish look in his eyes, I was exhausted from the calls, the texts, and the stalking. For a second, I considered agreeing to go with him. Then, I remembered the call I received from my cousin earlier that day. I remembered my girls and how they'd feel knowing they had to live with him again.

I changed my mind.

'Leave me alone,' I said, tearfully.

A few minutes later, he stood up and left.

When I got back to my hotel room, hours later, I got a call from my mother — she wanted to know how I was doing. I told her that he showed up at the dance class. She asked if I listened to what he had to say. When I said no, she got upset with me and started to scold me. She told me I was stubborn and I was derailing from God's plan for my life. She complained that I wasn't giving him a chance, and that was not Christ-like of me.

'You are being stubborn, and you are listening to advice from people who don't care about you!' she yelled.

My heart sank. All I had ever wanted was to do right by my mum. When I got off the call with her, I sent him a text message giving him a time and place to meet up.

*

When he came to my table at The Place, Victoria Island, I had the recorder on my phone on — hoping he'd say something incriminating. But he didn't. Instead, he started to act weird, like a drug addict. He said he was not feeling well because he hadn't seen me in a while. I asked if he would tell me all that happened with him and Blessing, but he insisted that she lied against him and nothing ever happened.

He then said, 'I have a favour to ask you.'

'Go ahead.'

'Can we please make love? I am not feeling well, and I know once we have sex, I will feel better,' he said, leaning in towards me.

I was dumbfounded, to say the least. Eventually, I found my voice.

'No, you can go and have sex with other women. You have my permission.'

'You are the only one I want. Please help me.'

'No.'

He looked shocked that I had turned him down.

My phone beeped. My Uber had arrived. 'I need to leave. My Uber is here.'

'Okay. Can I ask for another favour?'

'No, you can't drop me with your car,' I responded before he got the chance to word his next favour. I didn't want him to know my location and start to stalk me there.

I left him at the table to join my Uber driver. After a few minutes of being in the Uber, I felt a prick on my neck, so I looked back instinctively. I saw his car following my Uber. As soon as I realised this, I asked the Uber to stop close to a police stand; then, I got out of the car to confront him and ask him to stop following me. He apologised and promised to stop stalking me.

I got back in my Uber and continued to monitor him. Soon, he stopped at a junction, pretending to make a left turn. A few seconds later, he was back on our trail.

'I don't know why this man is following me o,' I complained to the Uber driver.

'Do you know him?' the Uber driver asked.

'No oo,' I lied. 'I met him at the restaurant. He asked for my number and I said no and now he is just following me everywhere.'

'Haba. I don't like men like this. You have already told him no.'

'Please can we lose him?'

'Yes. Don't worry.'

The Uber driver took several turns until we lost him, and I was able to breathe easy. The moment I got to the hotel, I gave the hotel management his plate number and car colour, and begged them not to let him in.

A few minutes later, I got a mail from him.

Don't Do it

3 Aug

to me

Seyi,

That you said I can have sex with anybody
does not mean I allow you to have sex with
anyone.

I am the one and only sex partner for you.

You having sex with someone else will make
me angry and will be a sin against me, my
head, against the law and against God.

Please don't do it cos the meeting you have
is with a guy in your hotel room.

We are legally married and sex outside
marriage is an offense.

Regards
Your hustand

I was disgusted at the fact that he thought I had time to sleep with other men, after literally just running away from an abusive marriage.

These days, every time I think of the time he trailed my Uber ride, I shudder.

As I write this, I shudder.

I didn't see the big picture that day. Although, I didn't get into his car because I didn't want him to know where I was staying, I somehow missed the fact that if I had entered his car, he could have killed me, and that would have been the end. Nobody knew I was meeting with him. I went because I wanted to please my mum, but I didn't tell her I was meeting him that day.

I thank my stars that I didn't get into his car that day.

He would continue to send me tons of emails and text messages, after that day, threatening me. When I accused him of harassing me, he turned tables and skewed the course of events; like when he called my elder brother to tell him I was harassing him and his family.

When my CNN African Voices feature aired, my dad called me to inform me that my ex-husband's mother had called him to say my ex said people were threatening him — and I was one of them. I was very irritated by the call; mostly by the fact that someone said this to my dad and he believed it.

How jobless could I have been?

'Daddy, Google my name please. So, you can see that I am a great woman who has no time for such frivolities.'

That same evening, I got a message from his sister. She claimed I was harassing her brother and promised that I'd see their wrath if I didn't stop and stay away from their family. The last sentence of her message read, 'Those who live in glass houses don't throw stones.'

On some days, I'd get calls and when I said hello, there would be no response.

I was scared and confused. But I was unable to change my main phone line because it was also my work line that a lot of people had associated with Dream Catchers.

Eventually, when I realised they were only projecting their fears onto me, I blocked every member of his family.

*

It was Ann Taylor, who wrote the famous poem, one of my all-time favourites, '*Who sat and watched my infant head, while sleeping on my cradle bed, and tears of sweet affection shed? My mother.*'

When you are ill and you need someone to lean on, who is the first person your mind goes to? For me, it's usually my mum. Whenever I am in a fix or confused, she is the one I always want to run to — although I almost never do that.

The one time when I needed my mother the most — when I was weak, having just escaped being murdered and still being bullied by a manipulative man and his family — she was not there.

On the night of the day I left the house, when I informed my parents that I would not be honouring Toba's father's invitation to be interrogated at his house, my mother suggested my father attend on my behalf. When my father refused to go, my mother invited Toba to the house to talk things through.

Despite hearing my side of things and snippets from my father, my mother (who was not in the country at the time) insisted on hearing from Toba and his family, because according to her, 'nobody was there'. It shocked me that my mother was insistent on hearing another 'side of the story', when I, her daughter, had recounted my traumatic experience to her, several times.

After a while, I decided to have another call with her, to explain the pain I was going through and how Toba had been falsely accused of rape in the past. I also told her of how he would borrow money many times, promising to pay back, but never making good his word.

It was at this point that my mother told me, 'He said he bought you a property with his money.'

My mouth fell wide open. I quickly collected myself and refuted the claim.

'He should come and say it to my face!' I responded, shocked and angry. 'He knows I am the one who made a down payment for a property in both our names.'

'No. His mother said the treasury money, only ₦500, ooo is his own but that he used everything to buy you the property.'

I was shocked at this revelation. This treasury money was one of the things that gave me the courage to marry him even though he was broke and jobless. I had believed he had savings that he could re-invest and he wouldn't need to use all of my money — if push came to shove.

'He told me he lent his brother all that money,' I told my mother. I hoped that she would finally see him for the pathological liar that he truly was.

'You know what you will do? Call his mother and explain that he didn't buy you any property.'

I agreed to this. At this point, I felt like my mum and I were close to being on the same page.

I called his mother. She responded with her usual calm voice, clearly hoping that I had finally agreed to go back home.

After a few pleasantries, I said to her, 'Mummy, what Blessing is saying, I believe it because he has told me in the past that someone falsely accused him of rape.'

'Is it an issue of over three years that you are now bringing up? Is that why you are dragging the Blessing issue?' She said, dismissively, in Yoruba, her voice remaining calm as ever.

'It is a big issue ma. Also, I heard that he said he bought me a property. He did not buy me anything. I am the one that used my money for a down payment for a property in both our names.'

She was quiet for a beat.

Then she said, 'I have heard you. What we need to focus on now, is how to resolve this issue.' The nonchalance in her voice is not something I will ever forget. As I write, it rings in my ear.

For the longest time, I called myself a lot of demeaning names because I was stupid enough to get a property and put both our names on it.

*

There are two things I have found most painful about my mother's involvement in this entire situation; the first being Blessing staying at my parent's house. My dance studio was at their house, so I'd often run into her.

Once, I called my mother on phone and asked, 'Does Blessing have to live in your house?'

'Why do you ask?' she replied.

'Because every time I see her, my heart gets broken all over again.'

'Well, only the Holy Spirit can tell me what to do with her,' she replied.

'Okay,' I responded, and ended the call.

The second hit me shortly after my mother returned to Nigeria, a few months after my separation. She asked me over for a visit and I obliged. I had been in her room for a few minutes when Blessing appeared. Apparently, my mother had set up a 'mediation session' without my knowledge or consent. I resolved to remain calm through the meeting.

'Any time I greet Aunty Seyi, she will tell me not to greet her,' Blessing said, in the course of the 'mediation session'. I really wanted to slap the words out of her mouth, as soon as they came out. My mother shifted her focus to me.

'Is that true?'

'Yes ma,' I responded. 'I don't need her greeting.'

Eventually, Blessing left the room and my mother asked to hear some of the things that happened with Toba and Blessing, again. I explained to her in as much detail as possible. I still nursed the hope that if I talked to her in person, she would finally understand that my life was really in danger and then, she would be on my side. I was wrong.

After I finished speaking, she said to me, 'Your marriage failed because you lied to me when you wanted to move out of Ikorodu. If you had not lied to me, your husband would have loved and cherished you. But you lied to me. Your relationship with him was therefore built on a lie.'

I didn't need to hear any more. I quietly escaped into my shell and accepted that I would never have my mother by my side on this issue; she would always think it was my fault that my husband stole from me and tried to murder me.

CHAPTER ELEVEN

I DID GO TO THE POLICE

"Domestic violence has often gone unnamed and unblamed in my society. It is the norm for men to teach their wives a lesson, and for the women to bear that beating and teaching with no complaints."
— Fatima Mohammed

The first time I went to the police was when I wrote my initial flimsy statement on July 15, just a few minutes after I had left the house. The police station was close to where we lived, and we often passed by it on our way home, but I never thought I'd have cause to visit. Yet, there I was.

After I had scribbled a few incoherent words that afternoon, I remember the lady in charge asking me to write the truth so they could pick him up, before the story got mixed up. She kept saying, 'Na person wey first come police get case. Make we go carry this man before he scatters the thing.'

But I didn't listen. Why would I give up the man I married, who had claimed to love me? The man who would come back begging! I didn't listen.

And in truth, I regretted this decision. I still regret it.

I had been gone from the house for a few weeks. At this point, I had no clothes or anything of value on me. My foster kids had no clothes either. We recycled clothes and underwear.

I was afraid to go to the house to pick up my things. I had watched so many Investigation Discovery Extra episodes with him, that I feared he'd set the house on fire with me in it if I ever entered that house again.

I spoke to a few people about my dilemma and my need to get my belongings, and I was advised to go through a domestic violence non-profit organisation. I agreed to this.

When I arrived at the office of the non-profit organisation, I was asked to fill out a form; then, narrate my story to their representatives. I told them all I wanted was to be able to get my belongings from the house and maybe file a restraining order. The representatives said they would work on this. I felt relieved, until I was told that I'd have to go back to the police station to write a proper statement.

It was tiresome to think I had to return to the police station. I contemplated possible alternatives, there were none. So, a few days later, I put on my big-girl pants and headed to the same police station where I had written the first statement — accompanied by my sister and her husband. They stayed in the car.

I was going to write another one, but first I was asked to narrate the course of events to the policewoman in charge of the gender unit. I did. When I finished, she blamed me for letting a girl stay in my house while I was married; as if I had married an animal who had no self-control. Somehow, I – the lady and victim, was to be blamed for the man's infidelity, and it seemed stupid to me.

I really wanted to tell her off and, probably, educate her on how it is the society that enables men by blaming women for the terrible actions that men commit. But, I am not one to offend an officer, so I swallowed my words and asked for the paper to pen down my statement.

As I finished writing my statement, the DPO walked in from an inner room and took a seat. At that same moment, a woman selling *amala* entered the building. The policewoman handed my written statement to the DPO, which he read while he bought *amala* and *ogunfe* from the seller. After a few minutes of scanning through the statement, he returned it to the policewoman, collected his *amala* from the vendor, and began to eat.

He had swallowed two morsels before he asked me in Yoruba, 'You are the one with this statement?'

I nodded.

'And you are sure you don't want to resolve this?'

'I am sure,' I responded.

'I am asking because once we start a police case and pick him up, there is no going back. Things could get dirty.'

'I know,' I responded.

He continued to eat. Then, he turned to me again.

'If we say this one is not good, and that one is not good, what will now be good for us? Husband is scarce o,' he said in Yoruba.

'I just want to get my things from the house,' I responded.

He asked for the address and I penned it down. He then asked if I wanted them to invite him to the station.

'Because he can say that you are lying and this thing will be a mess.'

The woman who attended to me on the 15th of July had walked into the room at this time.

'*Sebi* I tell you that day,' she whispered to me in pity.

I became terrified of the situation turning into a mess — of it becoming a social media scandal.

So, I said again, 'I just want to get my clothes. You can invite him.'

'Okay. No problem,' the DPO said. 'We will keep visiting the house to see if he is there. We will call you once we see him. Leave your number.'

I dropped my number and thanked him.

As I headed out, the woman from the gender unit followed me. 'You need to drop something for the work to go fast o.'

I gave her ₦5,000 but I never heard from them.

*

I got a call from the non-profit organisation some days later. They wanted to know if I had filed the police report and I answered in the affirmative.

They asked me to provide a copy of the report and said they could use it to help me get a restraining order. I was elated and relieved to hear this. My joy, however, sank to hopelessness when they told me I'd have to pay ₦50,000 to start the process of getting a restraining order.

I didn't have that much money at the time but I was happy to borrow from friends.

'When will the order be ready?' I asked.

'You have a 50/50 chance. There's the possibility of the judge turning down the request for a restraining order.'

I wasn't about to source for ₦50,000 on something whose outcome was not certain, so I stopped talking to them. I didn't think they could help me.

*

After a few months of living with my sister, I had saved up some money, which I used to rent a new place for myself and my foster kids. I decided, then, that it was time to face my fears and go to the old house to get the things I left behind.

To be safe, I hired three military men, with whom I went to the house. I also hired two trucks to carry my belongings.

When I got to the house, I was met with the biggest shock. He had changed all the locks to the house and I had no access. I spoke to my friend, a lawyer, who told me that I had the right to break the locks as it was also my house, but I was afraid I could get into trouble for doing that, so I didn't heed his advice. My sister and brother-in-law who had accompanied me also thought it best that I look for the key instead of breaking in.

I knew he was the only one who would have the key, which meant having to do what I had dreaded for months: contact him.

But I didn't want to call him, so I decided to go to his 'office', which was at the bottom flat of his father's house.

He was most likely going to be there — pretending to work.

I drove over with the military men but he wasn't at the office. My brother-in-law called him with a different number, pretending to want to make clothes, but he was able to figure out it was my brother-in-law, so he did not take the calls.

His absence seemed too convenient; we had reason to believe one of the security men at the estate had called him to inform him of our presence.

With all other options yielding no results, we went back to the house, where I resolved to do what I hated the most; I called him and asked that he come around to open the gate. I remember the conversation so well because it was one of the most difficult things I had ever had to do.

Unfortunately, we had more of an argument than a conversation. He blatantly refused to come to the house to open the gate.

Instead, he said, 'Go back to wherever you have been all these days.' After which, he asked me to call the lawyer who rented the house to us for the key.

I called the lawyer. 'Good evening sir. This is Seyi Oluyole, the tenant at the house in Magodo (*address withheld*).'

He seemed quite irritated the moment he heard my voice. 'Yes?! Why are you calling me?'

'Sir, I'd like to ask for the receipt to the house. I haven't gotten it since I paid the rent. And also, I heard the key to the gate is with you.'

'Do you think I'm stupid?' he asked.

I was too dumbfounded by the question to give an answer.

'Come to my office with your husband if you want to talk to me,' he said, and ended the call.

I turned to my sister in frustration, hot tears threatening to fall from my eyes.

That day, we returned home without my belongings. I had paid the truck drivers and military men for nothing.

Later that night, at my sister's house, my dad called me to ask why I went to the house with soldiers. 'You need wisdom for these things,' he said.

'How did you know I was at the house with military men?' I asked, knowing none of us had told him or my mother, because the plan was to get to the house unannounced.

It was that day I realised that they had been talking to this man, not caring that he tried to murder me. It was the same day I left the family group chat.

'I'd rather have no family than deal with this.'

Those were my last words on the group chat before I cried my eyes out, for the umpteenth time.

Much later, I called my lawyer friend to ask for his help in retrieving the key. He decided to call the lawyer who rented the house to me, at which point we were able to get him to bring the key to me without requiring my husband's presence.

It was also on this day that I found out that my husband had collected the receipt to the house a week after payment, and had even put his name on the receipt, although I had been the one to pay for the house. Never mind that I would confront him about having collected the receipt without informing me, days after, and he would deny it.

*

On the first day of a writer's workshop in September, the first since the incident, I saw Nkiru – also, for the first time since the incident. I gave her a massive hug.

But I was having the worst workshop ever, brought on by a mix of the worst panic attacks, and my inability to sleep at night. Colleagues asked to know how I was feeling and what the problem was but I couldn't express myself in coherent words; the last time I had been at that hotel, I was with him.

I spent many nights in Nkiru's room, hoping it would ease my insomnia. It did not.

After a particularly dreadful nightmare, I woke up in the middle of the night and came to the full realisation that the man I married had locked me up for a full day and attempted to kill me. I realised then that all I had been dealing with up until that point was his infidelity with Blessing. I hadn't processed the rest of it.

I started to have flashbacks of being locked up; the pillow over my face; my pool of tears as I begged him to let me out; how I was certain I was going to die.

I was losing my mind. I couldn't think. It was at this point I realised that I was ready to pursue a case against him. Eventually, I did another one of the things that I feared the most. I posted a tweet recounting the facts of what I went through on the 8th of July 2019. In minutes, the post had received a number of reactions – in the guise of support and castigations, with the support outweighing the vile comments.

Many people messaged me, old friends called; each of them, glad that they weren't getting news of my death.

Then, I received a message from someone promising to help me make sure that my ex-husband faced justice, if I followed his instructions. I was afraid it would turn into a Nigerian case – needlessly prolonged, excruciatingly expensive and altogether unresolved, but he was confident it would not. So, I agreed to pursue the case.

In the course of the next days, I visited the DSVRT, Domestic and Sexual Violence Response Team, where I picked up a letter, which I was asked to drop at the women's right office/gender unit of the police headquarters in Lagos.

Right before I walked into the police headquarters, I received a call from the agent whom I had liaised with to secure the property on which I put both our names. I explained to her that I was no longer in contact with him. She confirmed that she had called him and in light of things, even suggested to him that we split the property, but he was adamant.

'He would rather neither of us have it. And I have given up,' I told her in surrender, and ended the call immediately. Then, I walked into the station, hoping to at least get justice — which would mean I did not lose out completely.

I was asked to drop my phones before signing in, which I did.

I went up to the office I had been directed to, to submit the letter from the DSVRT. I also explained the incident to the officers, and they were shocked.

An officer was soon assigned to me.

When the officer reviewed the letter from the DSVRT, she said, 'This is an attempted murder case. We will summon him.'

Her assertion gave me confidence.

She took down my phone number and promised to call me the moment they reached him, and were able to fix a date. Then, she said, 'But you have to give me ₦5,000 for dispatch and then give me something to hold.'

I tried to explain to her that I didn't have a lot of money at the time, to no avail. I didn't leave her office until I had coughed up ₦6,000 and promised to do better the next time I came.

*

The afternoon she called, my heart skipped several beats before I answered.

'We have summoned your husband. So, he will be here on Thursday. You too come by 10:00 am.'

I was happy and confident of the outcome, but I needed someone to accompany me and I didn't have anyone in mind. So, I spoke to Nkiru's partner, who reached out to a friend and asked her to help me out. She agreed to go with me.

When I got to the police station that Thursday morning, right before I took the stairs to the office I had submitted the letter the other day, I saw my ex-husband. He was wearing a white shirt and he was without his afro — which he had probably gotten rid of in a bid to look 'responsible'. There was a man in a black suit with him.

As soon as I got upstairs, I couldn't see them anymore.

I went to the officer assigned to my case and greeted her, feeling confident that my assailant was going to sleep behind bars.

'How are you my dear? So, today we will deal with your case. They are going to try to help you settle it.'

On hearing those words, my heart sank.

'Settle what?' I asked. 'It's an attempted murder case.'

'It's a husband and wife case. Just wait outside,' she said.

I wanted to walk away, but I couldn't; the woman Nkiru's partner had asked to accompany me was running late.

I was waiting outside with other women, when a policewoman accosted me, yelling, 'What is this? What are you wearing?'

I was startled.

She continued to yell, 'You want to seduce all our men here? Men that are not enough? *Oya* be going! Go back to where you came from!'

Dumbfounded, I went back into the office to talk to my assigned officer. 'That woman is yelling and asking that I go home because of my clothes.'

She looked at my sleeveless jumpsuit and said, 'Next time wear something like suit.'

'I have a scarf,' I responded. Then, took my wine-coloured pashmina from my bag and made it into a jacket-like covering.

Then, I returned outside where I stood for hours before Nkiru's partner's friend arrived. A few minutes later, we were called into the office, but were told our companions were to remain outside, while me and him sat in for the meeting.

I deeply resented having to sit beside him. Knowing him well, I was prepared for him to try to gaslight me, and promised myself to remain calm.

The woman at the desk asked us to narrate what happened. He decided he'd go first and repeatedly referred to me as 'my wife' knowing full well that it would upset me — but I didn't give him the satisfaction of seeing my reaction. I sat quietly.

He said I had imagined all the incidents because I had a mental problem. The woman, shocked, turned to me.

'Is it true you have a mental problem?'

'No ma,' I replied, calmly.

She turned back to him. 'You, how do you know she has mental problem? Are you a doctor?'

'No, but she told me. I have all the evidence.' He spoke so fervently, trying his best to make me lose my cool. I was as calm as Beyoncé in the elevator.

I sat there, listening to him skew the reality of events that led up to the incident in a bid to make me look truly crazy — quiet, but mostly regretting that I had brought this case to the police. Who did I think I was, expecting that my case would be treated any differently?

He told different versions of the same story, defecting when questions were asked — so picturesque of a crazy person, himself, that the policewoman yelled at him several times, saying, 'Mr. Man I will arrest you o!'

She repeated the threat so many times, I began to wonder what the delay was about.

At one point, she told him, 'You have a problem and it means all what this woman is saying is true.'

Still, she did not try to make an arrest. The evidence was overwhelming — in how he was behaving like a loon, yet they didn't attempt to arrest him.

After the extended back and forth — with me sitting quietly, for the most part, willing the whole thing to end — I was asked what I wanted. This was my chance to ask for a repayment of all my money, and even request that he return my property documents, but I didn't care about all that anymore.

'Just tell him to leave me alone. And he should write a statement that nothing must happen to me.' That was all I said. That was all I wanted.

'What if she commits suicide?' he quickly asked the policewoman.

'Nothing must happen to her. You will write it!' the policewoman replied, in anger.

Right then, our companions were ushered in. It was at that point I realised that the man, who was supposedly his uncle, was also a lawyer.

My companion turned to me to say she had to leave in a hurry.

When she left, the policewoman who had been attending to us handed me a ₦100 note and asked me to get her a bottle of water while my ex wrote his statement.

I don't know what I was thinking, but I actually took the money and left her with my ex and his lawyer uncle, to get her the water. When I returned with the bottle of water, the office was empty.

I went to my assigned officer.

'He has written his statement that he will leave you,' she said.

I nodded in defeat and left. I didn't even ask to see the statement. I was exhausted.

When I got home that evening, I wept. I wept so hard. I felt truly and completely defeated.

I wished I had never tried to get justice.

AUTHOR'S NOTE

I started writing this book in September 2019. In the beginning, it was just me journaling, in a desperate attempt to not lose my mind. Everything that happened had left me in shock; and with each passing day, even more events unfolded, leaving me completely numb.

Writing helped me cope.

Then, it became a vendetta. The pain I was feeling was too much — I wanted him to pay. Since going to the police yielded nothing, I decided to exact my revenge by writing a tell-all book, so that the world would know about this evil man. He would suffer for his sins, and no woman would ever want to be with him again.

But I always hit a roadblock. I would get too emotional and stop. Reliving the entire event was traumatic — I couldn't write it.

Eventually, I left the document on my laptop, uncertain I was ever going to revisit, let alone finish, it.

Days passed, then weeks, and then months. I began to realise that there are many terrible people in the world, and nothing I could write would exact the revenge I sought. I couldn't get back the months I lost with him. I couldn't get back the deals he talked me out of. I couldn't stop another woman from falling victim to him — more importantly, it wasn't my responsibility.

Gradually, I came to the realisation that my quest for vendetta was making me a prisoner to him; a slave to my trauma. There was no way I could get better, move on, because I was filled with so much rage and fear.

I needed to find healing for myself and stop worrying about his next victim. I needed to stop giving him control over my decision-making.

Also, I knew I had to be careful — he had stated once that I was mentally ill, and he would not hesitate to portray future events in the same light, just to gaslight me. Heck! That was probably what he had to say to friends who got curious enough to question him.

I did not come back to this book for months. At that time, I no longer cared about vendetta or vengeance, or even about releasing it on my 29th birthday.

I cared about me: about my healing, and controlling my panic attacks.

One time, I got so scared and triggered that I went to hide in my wardrobe, shivering. I needed to be able to manage events like this. So, I began to focus on my healing.

I told my editor I couldn't cope with writing the book and it was comforting to know she understood; she asked me to take my time. By March 2020, I had stopped writing and journaling altogether.

But I have always wanted to write a book. I had a book deal once, but I never published the book. I wanted to do something special for my 30th birthday.

Then, March 2021 rolled around. And I decided to resume writing this book.

Why? Because I am a writer and a storyteller — and this is the story I have chosen to tell.

This is my story — told by me, for me, at my own time.

I might sound inspiring but trust me when I say I am still a messed-up work-in-progress. I can go from having a great day to getting triggered by the most frivolous thing, and my day is ruined.

I second-guess myself a lot — and I have to inhale and exhale repeatedly to remind myself of my confidence and genius.

Hurt people hurt others, so I am constantly checking myself to make sure I didn't pick any gaslighting traits.

There are days where I have to sit and try to remember events, just to be sure they truly happened.

Anything triggers me — a social media post, a car model, a perfume smell, being accused of dishonesty — anything! Sometimes, it's my regret. I would be so neck deep in regrets, I would wish I could turn back the hands of time. Like when I remember a call I received from a representative of the Ooni of Ife in 2019, a few days after I had run out of the house, to receive an award of achievement/recognition. I was supposed to follow up with certain details, leading up to the recognition ceremony, but my mind had been too muddled to hold on to anything other than the pain and anxiety I felt at the time – so much so, I could not attend the event and, therefore, forfeited the award. Now, every year, when I see other recipients of this award, I get so sad. And this, is just one of many things I regret.

I haven't picked up my National ID card because I am still scared of running into his sister at that building.

And as at the time of completing this book, I haven't forgiven myself.

On some days, I feel like nothing. I feel like a worthless piece of crap that wasn't good enough for her husband; wasn't good enough for her parents to defend her; and isn't good enough for anyone or any love.

On many other days, I see myself for who I really am: a queen, worthy of love and respect, and deserving of a healthy love life and healthy, loving relationships.

On many days, I feel strong and powerful.

Finding the balance is hard.

Trying to stay grateful is difficult, still I try.

One thing I know for sure is that things have gotten a lot better. Time did heal some wounds. In the heat of all this, I wrote a note to myself, and now when I read it, I realise how much growth I have achieved:

Hi Seyi,

If you are alive, it means you weathered the storm and that bastard didn't get you.

How are you? And how have you fared these past few years? I hope you've finally been able to get through the pain that (name withheld) put you through?

Did it become a huge social media/ press scandal where you had to come out to defend yourself? I really hope it didn't. And if it did happen, I hope you trumped that bastard and came out stronger.

Have you been able to forgive him? If you have, wow! Wow!

Have you run into him at any time, and how did you feel?

How many times have you and your babies travelled the world to dance? Have you met Rihanna yet? Beyoncé? Serena? Whom have you met? And are you now a member of the UN? Did Seun finally grow tall? ... Hahahahaha!

Please keep loving yourself and if you are not there yet, keep working on it.

Did you meet someone new? Hahahahaha ... bad joke, I know. I am so sorry for all the pain you had to go through starting from that day, July 8th, and I'm hoping it has made you greater like everyone said it would.

Well done for all you do. Learn that pole dancing and remember that if it seems too good to be true, it probably is.

I wrote this book for me.

ACKNOWLEDGEMENTS

Sister Mi and Engineer, when the chair was pulled from underneath me, you had my back. You fought for me at every point! I am blessed to call you family. I love you!

Ijeoma, remember how I'd always smile widely every time I saw you, and you'd ask, 'why are you always smiling when you see me?' This book is why. You waited - you were there. Thank you. I'll still have that huge smile every time I see you!

The Ogwuegbu Family, you are a rock to the world! Thank you for opening your home to a scared 28-year-old and her 10 children. THANK YOU!

Ayodeji Osowobi, I often remember the first day we met at that Guardian shoot and I wish to turn back to hands of time — just so I can take our connection seriously; in hopes that our friendship would have saved me from so many terrible choices. Nonetheless, I called you right after the incident, and you were there. Thank you.

Modupe Rahmon, thank you for your wisdom - you followed me to so many offices to help me feel safe, you picked up the slack when I couldn't.

To my brothers, for having my back. Dami, for calling and telling me not to go back, no matter what. Sean, I still remember how you flipped. Mostly, I remember that you said 'Seyi, your girls are watching you. If you go back, they'll think it's okay to be treated badly by men.'

Deborah Eijah, thank you for that phone call on that Saturday morning. Thank you for doing your best.

My Dream Catchers Academy babies, DCA FOREVER! LIKE THE PHOENIX, WE WILL RISE!

Made in the USA
Coppell, TX
21 July 2023